MW00466936

If you find this book, either
enjoy it yourself or return to...

_____

_____

_____

_____

Published by LifeWay Press®
© 2012 LifeWay Press

ISBN: 978-1-4158-7238-3
Item: P005474749

Dewey Decimal Classification Number: 248.6
Subject Heading: PERSONAL FINANCES \ STEWARDSHIP \ TIME MANAGEMENT \ CONSERVATION OF NATURAL RESOURCES

Printed in the United States of America.

Young Adult Ministry Publishing
LifeWay Church Resources
One LifeWay Plaza
Nashville, Tennessee 37234-0135

We believe that the Bible has God for its author; salvation for its end; and truth, without any mixture of error, for its matter and that all Scripture is totally true and trustworthy. To review LifeWay's doctrinal guideline, please visit *www.lifeway.com/doctrinalguideline.*

Cover design by Heather Wetherington

TABLE OF CONTENTS

ABOUT THE AUTHORS

FRED "CHIP" LUTER III

Chip ("Stewarding God's Money" and "Building Healthy Relationships") is youth and young adult pastor at Franklin Avenue Baptist Church in New Orleans, Louisiana, where his father is pastor. He's married to the love of his life, Jasmine, and they reside in Metairie, Louisiana. A native of New Orleans, Chip is a proud member of the Who Dat Nation. (Go Saints!)

Chip began his journey as a minister of the gospel at Dallas Baptist University. While there, he served as a resident assistant, president of the Black Student Union, and vice president of the Student Government Association. When he's not ministering to teens and young adults, you can find Chip eating bowls of his momma's famous gumbo.

MICAH CARTER

Micah ("Discerning Our Days" and "Ruling the Earth") is publishing team leader for Threads, the young adult ministry at LifeWay Christian Resources in Nashville, Tennessee. He's married to Meredith, and they have two "sons of thunder": Benjamin and Jonathan. He and his family live in Franklin, Tennessee, where they are members of ClearView Baptist Church.

Micah enjoys reading, studying theology, playing golf, collecting fountain pens, fishing, and is passionate about Asian cuisine. But most of all, he loves spending time with family and friends, particularly when there's coffee to be shared. And, he's part Samoan, even though he doesn't look it.

Created to Care

What it means to watch over all God has given us

Stewardship. It's one of those old, churchy words you probably don't hear often—but it's a word ripe with meaning and purpose. *Merriam-Webster's Collegiate Dictionary* defines *stewardship* as "the conducting, supervising, or managing of something; *especially* the careful and responsible management of something entrusted to one's care." This definition hits the nail on the head: a steward is a manager of someone else's resources.

The biblical foundation for stewardship recognizes everything we have comes from God and, consequently, we're responsible to care for all He has entrusted to us. First Corinthians 4:2 says, "it is expected of managers that each one of them be found faithful." Without a doubt, God expects us to be faithful managers of all He's placed in our care.

Although stewardship is often connected with money, and for good reason, there's much more for us to manage with our lives beyond the financial. In this study, we'll examine four key areas that demand responsible management: money, time, relationships, and the environment. The Bible has much to say about each of these, not the least of which is the truth they point us back to: God is the Creator and Provider of everything.

Money, time, relationships, and the environment are in our care. How will we faithfully manage each of them appropriately and leverage them for God's mission and kingdom?

How to Use This Book

What better way to learn about stewardship than in community with others? That's why we've designed *Manage* as a small group Bible study. Geared for a no-prep small group experience, this study is intended to be facilitator led with a strong discussion focus. In each session you'll find:

• Questions to help you and/or your group process the Scriptures and content of each session

• Facilitator tips (*) to help effectively lead the gathering

• A "This Week . . ." section at the close of each session to allow you to reflect on what was learned and put the session into practice in your personal life.

Stewarding God's Money

"Money won't make you happy . . .
but everybody wants to find out
for themselves."[1]   —Zig Ziglar

MONEY, MONEY, MONEY. It's everywhere—from get-rich-quick schemes to retailers pushing us to buy the latest and greatest gadget. It's easy to get pulled into the cultural message that making more money and buying more stuff will solve our problems. We're a culture of want, not need—of selfishness and instant gratification. The mantra of today is we *deserve* things and we deserve them right now.

(handwritten: What jobs do you want to have? Why?)

Money is fun. It's powerful, encouraging us to feel as though we have control over our lives. But our focus on money can quickly become ungodly if left unchecked:

(handwritten: Read)

> **"No one can serve two masters. Either you will hate the one and love the other, or you will be devoted to the one and despise the other. You cannot serve both God and Money"** (Matthew 6:24, NIV).

Why was money singled out in this passage instead of other idols? When are you more likely to "serve" money? What do you think it means to "serve" money?*

BANK ON IT
The ancient Greeks had only one word for bank: *trapezitai,* or "tables," which still serves today as their word for bank. Remind you of Jesus and a certain bank in the temple at Jerusalem (Matthew 21:12-13)?

> **"Don't you know that if you offer yourselves to someone as obedient slaves, you are slaves of that one you obey—either of sin leading to death or of obedience leading to righteousness"** (Romans 6:16)?

To what or whom are you daily offering yourself as a slave? Would you classify yourself as a slave to money? Why or why not?

How we approach money says a lot about who we are and what we stand for. If we focus solely on becoming rich, then our lives will be spent doing whatever it takes to earn wealth. However, this desire does not suit our

---

* Facilitator: Consider Luke 16:1-13. How does Jesus' parable of the dishonest manager/steward help us understand the high stakes of caring for what God has given to us?

design. We were not created for an infatuation with money, which can lead to destruction:

Read

> "For we brought nothing into the world, and we can take nothing out. But if we have food and clothing, we will be content with these. But those who want to be rich fall into temptation, a trap, and many foolish and harmful desires, which plunge people into ruin and destruction. For the love of money is a root of all kinds of evil, and by craving it, some have wandered away from the faith and pierced themselves with many pains" (1 Timothy 6:7-10).

Yikes. As Jesus said, "What does it benefit a man to gain the whole world yet lose his life?" (Mark 8:36). Mass accumulation of stuff gains us nothing. We can't take it with us when we die. Ultimately, God is the Source of our money, and He should be glorified with how we use it. Money is a gift from God:

> "God has also given riches and wealth to every man, and He has allowed him to enjoy them, take his reward, and rejoice in his labor. This is a gift of God . . ." (Ecclesiastes 5:19).

What do you think is meant by "take his reward" in this passage?

How we handle money says something about how we view God. Yielding to God with money—recognizing He's our Source—helps us yield to Him in other areas of our lives, like how we spend our time or what jobs we take.*

Managing money isn't a new concept; numerous passages in the Bible discuss being good stewards of our

---

CAN MONEY BUY HAPPINESS?

No . . . but also yes. God created us for relationships, and as scientific studies show, folks with close-knit relationships live longer, are healthier, and thrive more than those without.

So, while buying a new pair of shoes may make you pleased for a few days, buying a plane ticket to visit a friend or a dinner when you chow with buddies brings an ongoing, supportive sense of connection and, yes, happiness.

The key is spending on things that further your relationships, not stuff.

Ecclesiastes 5 explains that a life spent pursuing wealth is futile. It's better to get by with less money and to be able to enjoy our lives.

---

* **Facilitator:** Ask your group to reflect on their actions this week. Consider your own as well. What do those actions reveal as to who or what masters you? What would you like to change about your behavior? Pray for the Spirit to work mightily in them, and for them to lean on Him for help in altering whom they serve.

wallets. True, there aren't verses detailing 401ks, investment portfolios, rainy day funds, or choosing the right loan payment schedule. But the specifics aren't as necessary as the biblical principles. The Good Book offers two simple concepts for money management.

Try out this Amish axiom for contentment today: "Use it up, wear it out, make do, or do without."

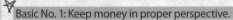
Basic No. 1: Keep money in proper perspective.

There's no doubt about it: Money is essential; it's our means of paying the bills, educating ourselves, and improving our circumstances. Money is a resource given by God to meet our needs, helping us toward an abundant life. But that abundance doesn't come from acquiring more and more wealth. Abundance is found in lives that are full of hope and joy, in relationships, in seeking God and doing His will.

We can have an abundance of income no matter our paycheck if we *manage* it well. The size of our paycheck matters less than what we do with it. We can poorly manage lots of money or a little bit of money. But it's in managing well that we find abundance and avoid ungodly and unhealthy extremes.

Our perspective on money is one major determinant of our faithfulness (or lack thereof) with the gifts God has given us:

SEDUCTION
From Latin's *seducere*, meaning "to persuade a vassal to desert his allegiance or service." Vassals were protected by their feudal lords to whom they'd sworn loyalty. Any similarities strike you here?

"Whoever is faithful in very little is also faithful in much, and whoever is unrighteous in very little is also unrighteous in much. So if you have not been faithful with the unrighteous money, who will trust you with what is genuine? And if you have not been faithful with what belongs to someone else, who will give you what is your own" (Luke 16:10-12)?*

On a day-to-day basis, what does faithfulness with money look like?

What changes would you like to make in how you manage your money?

---

* Facilitator: Ask your group: When you think of faithfulness, what ideas/words come to mind? Let them list their thoughts. Then ask how money fits into their ideas of faithfulness—does it work in that context? Why or why not? Would they choose another term for how they manage their finances?

Basic No. 2: Manage money according to God's principles.

God knows that we can't do this on our own, so He has given us principles in His Word to help us practically live out His perspective on money.

> "The worries of this age, the seduction of wealth, and the desires for other things enter in and choke the word, and it becomes unfruitful" (Mark 4:19).

Name some examples of "the worries of this age, the seduction of wealth, and the desires for other things." How often do you face these examples? Do you recognize them as Word-chokers when you see them?

What principles and/or philosophies guide the way you currently manage money?

We'll spend the remainder of this session diving into a few of God's principles for money management. Let's begin with perhaps the most difficult part—learning to be content with what we have.

CHALLENGING THE AMERICAN DREAM *What is this?*

The culture we live in screams the American Dream: *Work hard. Make money. Spend money. You deserve it.* However, God hasn't called us to focus on making and spending money. He wants us to find contentment in what we have and to use our resources to glorify Him.

Read Proverbs 30:8b-9: *Read*

> "Give me neither poverty nor wealth; feed me with the food I need. Otherwise, I might have too much and deny You, saying, 'Who is the LORD?' or I might have nothing and steal, profaning the name of my God."

This prayer is comparable to **JESUS' MODEL PRAYER** (Matthew 6:9-13). Both ask God's protection from temptation; both ask for basic needs; both are concerned with upholding God's honor. The indulgent person may become a liar and a mocker (Exodus 5:2); the destitute person may become a thief (Proverbs 6:30). The thief profanes God by implying that God can't provide.[2]

---

* **Facilitator:** Discuss as a group: Why is Basic No. 1 so hard to do in today's culture? What obstacles keep you from putting Basic No. 2 into practice?

**OTHER VERSES
ON WEALTH &
CONTENTMENT**
Matthew 19:21-26
1 Timothy 6:6
Hebrews 13:5

The author of this proverb is asking God to keep him on the middle ground of money management. He doesn't want to be too rich or too poor. He doesn't want to be in poverty— unable to afford the necessities of life—but he doesn't desire great wealth because he fears it'll cause him to reject the Lord. In other words, the more money he possessed, the more likely he would go from depending on God to depending on his wealth to save him.

We tend to think the wealthiest people of society use money—not God—as the remedy to their problems. Culture screams: *Are you lonely? Buy friends. Unhappy? Buy stuff. Insecure? Buy security. Unpopular? Buy people.* Our society can't fathom this middle ground of contentment; instead we're either wealthy or poor. We don't celebrate those who have just enough to pay their bills and take care of their families. Instead, we respond to extremes, admiring those who live luxuriously and pitying those who live on the streets.*

How would life change if our goals weren't to gain wealth or avoid poverty but were solely focused on following God's will?

CREATE A BUDGET
Budgets are as diverse as the people on this planet. Here's a very simple breakdown of how to allocate your take-home pay:
  10% Tithe
  10% Save
  25% Living Expenses
  35% Housing & Debt
  5% Give
  15% Invest/Pay Off
      Student Loans

The apostle Paul has given us the secret we've all needed to hear—the secret of contentment.

"I don't say this out of need, for I have learned to be content in whatever circumstances I am. I know both how to have a little, and I know how to have a lot. In any and all circumstances I have learned the secret of being content—whether well fed or hungry, whether in abundance or in need. I am able to do all things through Him who strengthens me" (Philippians 4:11-13).

What does being content mean to you? How does that compare with what Paul says in these verses?

---

* Facilitator: Read Matthew 19:21-26. Talk about Jesus' saying, "With men this is impossible, but with God all things are possible." The disciples had an elevated view of wealthy people as we often do. And Jesus points out that only God can change people and their attitude toward money. We can't do it in our own strength.

Contentment doesn't mean that you're satisfied with being poor or don't want to be successful. It simply means that you live within your limitations. You can live with much, and you can live with less. It doesn't matter what you have or don't have; with God you can make it work. He will provide for your needs.

Don't seek cash, clothes, and cars. When you have contentment, you can be a better steward of what God's entrusted to you and reap the rewards of putting your faith in Him.

BALANCING THE BOOKS

When it comes to practical money management, the most foundational aspect is establishing—and following—a budget. Budgeting allows us to meet goals and live within our means. When we give forethought to using our income, our decisions are more realistic and less impulsive. It's embarrassing to spend a lot of money on a car that can't be maintained because there's no money left to change the oil or replace bald tires. It's ridiculous to have closets full of new clothing and insufficient funds to pay the bills.*

Budgets have a dry, stifling reputation, but nothing could be further from the truth. Giving proper attention to our checkbooks gives us control over our resources and reveals areas where we're hemorrhaging cash—exposing sources of savings that can set us free to prepare for future problems and give to those in need. Budgeting allows us to have a more thorough outlook on what we're spending, helping us to honor God with how we use what He's entrusted to us.

Christians aren't called to handle our money like everyone else. To paraphrase author Dave Ramsey, everyone else is "buying things they don't need with money they don't have to impress people they don't like." Our society has a spend-now-save-later mentality. Believers cannot buy into this illogic. Christ wants us to have a more abundant life, which can't be lived under the thumb of mismanaged money.*

FREE ONLINE BUDGETING
Don't fear the budget; embrace it and the financial freedom of knowing where money's going. Try some online options to launch your budget:
- *mint.com*
- *readyforzero.com*
- *yodlee.com*
- *money.strands.com*
- *budgettracker.com*

CONDEMNED BY THE CLASSICS
In Dante's *Inferno*, the fourth circle of Hell is reserved for hoarders (lusting after wealth) and wasters (spending too freely). Dante helpfully introduces the classical idea of moderation (the golden mean) in this level.

---

* Facilitator: A wise adage regarding possessions says: "Use things, love people. Not the other way around." What negative results occur when we mix these up? What wisdom can we glean from this?

FINANCIAL WORRYWART

Why do we worry? When it comes down to it, there are a limited number of things over which we have any control in our lives. When tough times come, put down your worry and pick up your prayer.

Ask God for opportunities and then do the leg work: Search your network for income options. Do your part to be a responsible manager of His blessings: Tithe what you can and cut back unnecessary spending.

Read Proverbs 24:3-4:

"A house is built by wisdom, and it is established by understanding; by knowledge the rooms are filled with every precious and beautiful treasure."

What essentials of financial planning can we learn from these verses?

One of the tenets of business school is "You manage what you measure." If you're not currently budgeting, what's keeping you from establishing one? If you do, how does having a budget make you feel?

[handwritten: What are ways we honor God w/ $? — tithe — now we use what we are given]

Every person's financial situation will dictate different needs, but all budgets have some similar categories: Tithing, Contributing, Conserving, and Consuming. Let's go through each one step-by-step.

TITHING: HONORING OUR SUSTAINER

A tithe is a 10 percent return on the investment God has made in our lives. (For many, 10 percent is a great, clear starting point.) It's our way of honoring Him for what He's given us by giving back a portion to Him. Tithing is essential for many reasons, but we'll focus on two:

1. Tithing gives back to God what is already His.

We financially support our priorities. As vital as we think some things are, our top financial priority is to remember who our financial gifts have come from and to allow Him to work through our contribution:

> **"You may say to yourself, 'My power and my own ability have gained this wealth for me,' but remember that the LORD your God gives you the power to gain wealth"** (Deuteronomy 8:17-18a).

[handwritten: Read]

---

* **Facilitator:** Ask your group to consider their honest attitude toward the money they earn. Do they really consider it as God's or as their own? What might change their perspective?

"Honor the LORD with your possessions and with the first produce of your entire harvest; then your barns will be completely filled, and your vats will overflow with new wine" (Proverbs 3:9-10).

How does tithing honor God? What are the rewards for tithing? Does tithing (or not tithing) affect your personal walk with God?

Tithing is mentioned in the Bible as early as Genesis 14:18-20.

2. Tithing allows us to join God in His work.

In the Old Testament, the biblical mandate to tithe was how Israel's priests and poor were cared for (Ezekiel 44:30). Today, tithing allows us to support our church leaders, missionaries, children's ministries, and so much more. In the New Testament, Jesus calls us all to give sacrificially as He leads *and* to practice justice and love:

> "But woe to you Pharisees! You give a tenth of mint, rue, and every kind of herb, and you bypass justice and love for God. These things you should have done without neglecting the others" (Luke 11:42).

Why was Jesus angry with the religious leaders in the temple?

Jesus expressed here that the way we spend money represents our love for Him and for others. Tithing must accompany consideration for and love of others. God is love, and all that He does comes from His love for us. We sacrifice a portion of our money for God and for the burdens of others as a testament to His love and sacrifice for us.

---

* Facilitator: Read Malachi 3:8-12. How do we often rob God today?

CONTRIBUTING: A THEOLOGY OF GENEROSITY

God is not against money. We use money for food, clothing, shelter, electricity, running water, education, vacation, and so forth. As much as we use money to support these necessities and desires, we also need it to participate in God's generosity.

Read James 1:17:

> "Every generous act and every perfect gift is from above, coming down from the Father of lights; with Him there is no variation or shadow cast by turning."

 When has God shown generosity to you?

God is generous. He has given us many gifts, including Jesus, who was generous with the people He encountered on earth. It's interesting to note that Jesus never lived as the wealthiest and most prosperous man— even though He was God in the flesh. Jesus taught us through His actions what it means to spend our lives being generous, looking not only to our needs, but to others' as well.*

Compare this verse with the story of Ruth and Boaz, and Deuteronomy 24:19: "When you reap the harvest in your field, and you forget a sheaf in the field, do not go back to get it. It is to be left for the foreigner, the fatherless, and the widow, so that the LORD your God may bless you in all the work of your hands."

One of my (Chip's) favorite sermons is the Sermon on the Mount, wherein Jesus challenges the people to switch their focus from keeping the letter of the law to growing a heart like His. Matthew 5:42 says,

"Give to the one who asks you, and don't turn away from the one who wants to borrow from you."

Jesus doesn't say specifically what needs to be given. He bases what needs to be given on what the person asks for.

We can't assume we'll always know how others need to be blessed; we just need to put ourselves in the position to be generous.

---

* Facilitator: Discuss ways your group can be generous to those in need on a consistent basis. Name some obvious needs you see in a typical week or month.

How do you typically respond when you see an obvious need? What attitudes or obstacles prevent you from meeting (even part of) a need?*

Read 2 Corinthians 9:6-13:

> "Remember this: The person who sows sparingly will also reap sparingly, and the person who sows generously will also reap generously. Each person should do as he has decided in his heart—not reluctantly or out of necessity, for God loves a cheerful giver. And God is able to make every grace overflow to you, so that in every way, always having everything you need, you may excel in every good work. As it is written:
>
> He scattered;
> He gave to the poor;
> His righteousness endures forever.
>
> Now the One who provides seed for the sower and bread for food will provide and multiply your seed and increase the harvest of your righteousness. You will be enriched in every way for all generosity, which produces thanksgiving to God through us. For the ministry of this service is not only supplying the needs of the saints, but is also overflowing in many acts of thanksgiving to God. They will glorify God for your obedience to the confession of the gospel of Christ, and for your generosity in sharing with them and with others through the proof provided by this service."

How is giving an act of "thanksgiving to God" (v. 11)?

Other Verses on Giving
Deuteronomy 15:7-8; 16:17
Nehemiah 5:10
Psalms 37:25-26; 112:5-6
Proverbs 28:27
Mark 12:41-44
Luke 6:34-36,38
Acts 20:35

---

* Facilitator: Discuss God providing for our needs. Ask your group how they feel about famine, contaminated water sources, and other causes of starvation in the world. Do they feel as though God should snap His fingers and fix the devastation? What if they are the means God chooses to use to fight hunger? How might they respond to that assignment?

The main point is this: When you give a lot, you receive a lot. This is not the same as prosperity theology. Attitude is key when it comes to giving: Either you have an open hand or a closed fist. The closed fist keeps what's inside, but nothing else can ever be added. The open hand is ready to let go of anything inside as well as receive anything new. God wants us to have an open hand when it comes to money, letting things go and letting Him use us more for His glory.

The bent of our sinful nature compels us to hoard, not to give. How can we become cheerful givers?

Consider the widow's gift in Luke 21:1-4. Jesus isn't concerned with the amount as much as He is with the heart of the gift. It's easy for someone to give out of what makes sense, but when our giving involves risk, it's faith.

Have you ever given beyond what you could spare to help others? To the church? What was the result?

Why don't we take more God-approved risks with our money? What makes something a God-approved risk?

As soon as we get paid, a portion of our funds should go first to Him. Then we should save for a purpose.

_____

CONSERVING: SAVE FOR A RAINY DAY

It's not hard to make an argument for saving money. Everyone knows we should do it, but making it a reality is difficult even though we know emergencies happen and that the future requires some big purchases. Eventually, your tire will go flat, you will get sick, you'll want a house that requires a down payment and repairs, and maybe, just maybe, you'll want to retire before turning 90.

Saving isn't just a solid financial principle. It's biblical:

> **"On the first day of the week, each of you is to set something aside and save in keeping with how he prospers, so that no collections will need to be made when I come"** (1 Corinthians 16:2).

How are we to save?

A wise person recognizes the financial pitfalls of not saving and plans ahead. We mainly save our money for three reasons: emergencies, large purchases (like a house, car, computer, or tuition), and retirement. We also like to plan ahead for things like vacation, braces, tuition payments, and unexpected medical bills.

What are your short-term savings goals?

QUICK TIPS FOR SAVING MONEY

Want to know the quickest way to save money? Stop spending what you already have. Here are six ways to save:

• Consistently choose a gas station that charges five cents a gallon less than one you prefer, and you'll save around $80 a year. Try *gasbuddy.com* for help.

• If you wear acrylic nails, start using your own nails and doing your own manicures. You could save an average of $520 a year.

• Switch to drinking water with your meals just once a week and you can save around $104 a year.

• Most people pay a cell phone bill of at least $50 a month ($600 a year). By switching to a prepaid phone, you can buy a 1,000-minute card for $100, then limit yourself to 100 minutes a month. You'll save $480 a year.

• Satellite or cable TV costs an average of $50+ a month. Is a year's TV-watching worth $600? Your local library isn't just books. They have all the latest movies available and books on CD—for free.

• Unless you really need the Internet in your home, why pay for it at all? Your local library offers free Internet access. If you do want this service at home but don't need it for work purposes, why pay more than you have to? Most people pay around $30 a month. Shop for bargains.

What have all these simple suggestions saved you in five years? More than $10,000. And what have you missed out on? Not much of anything.[3]

What are your long-term savings goals?

Take time to determine a plan to achieve those goals. Who do you know who could help guide you (a friend, person at church, financial planner, etc.)?

God promises to provide for us. However, we're to be good stewards of what He's given us and save for the future. Even if you can't save much every month, save what you can. Slow but steady wins the race.

Reviewing your spending habits is likely the best way to find extra for giving and saving. Let's take some time to examine our consumption.

CONSUMING: SPENDING WISELY

When our giving and saving are in order, they keep everything else in perspective. Understanding what needs to be given first helps us differentiate between our needs and wants. For example, I would like a new cell phone (even though I've had my current one for a year and there's nothing wrong with it). After I get paid, give my tithe, and put some money away in savings, I may not have enough to get that phone and take care of groceries, gas, and bills.

Now I have a decision to make: Is this new phone that necessary? If I choose to get it, what other area will suffer? Will I shortchange God? Forget about saving for my future?

The Bible has much to say about wasteful and wreckless spending. Here are a couple verses:

Spending & Debt Stats

- In 1950, the average new house was less than 1,000 sq ft; in 2000, the average new house was more than 2,000 sq ft.[4]

- About 70 percent of Americans are in debt.[5]

- The national debt in America continues to rise. Currently, each person's share is almost $51,000.[6]

"The plans of the diligent certainly lead to profit, but anyone who is reckless certainly becomes poor" (Proverbs 21:5).

"Watch out and be on guard against all greed because one's life is not in the abundance of his possessions" (Luke 12:15).

Examine your spending habits. Where is there excess that could be considered greed? What's one habit you'd like to change?

Take time this week to examine the percentage you spend on discretionary items verses giving and saving. Are you pleased with the results? Why or why not?

In the Parable of the Lost Son (Luke 15:11-32), we learn of a son who asks for his inheritance and squanders it. It's easy to point fingers at others who make poor financial decisions, but it often takes ample self-reflection to identify our own financial pitfalls.

What's the difference between needs and wants? Identify one area where you've possibly confused the two. What can you do with that money to better serve Christ?

RECOVERING FROM CON$UMPTION

Here are a few practical ways to let go of the false beliefs of our consumer culture.

- **Don't view yourself as the owner of anything**— whether it be your time, talents, or money. You and your stuff belong to God 86,400 seconds a day.
- **Make a personal goal to move down, not up, in lifestyle.** When we live below our means, we have more to give away (Ephesians 4:28).
- **Increase your giving.** As you earn more money, raise the amount you give to others.
- **Stop buying new cars.** Period.
- **Limit your exposure to "me-driven" media.** Try a media fast for one week every month or set a weekly limit on the number of hours you'll watch TV or surf the 'net.

For inspiration to change the world one step at a time, check out these great books: *Crazy Love* by Francis Chan, *Radical* by David Platt, or *Abide* by Jared C. Wilson.[7]

* **Facilitator:** Discuss ways your group members can eliminate $25 in spending each month. Talk about programs they'd like to donate to. What would motivate them to continue saving?

When a girl has the opportunity to go to school, she's . . .
• three times less likely to acquire HIV/AIDS
• will earn 25 percent more income in her life
• will have a healthier, better educated family.

Just $10 provides one girl with a year's supply of notebooks, pens, and pencils to support her learning and move toward a better future.

Learn more at *thehungersite.com*.[8]

If you were able to spend even $10 less per week and allocate that to charitable giving each month, where would you send the money? How could that change someone else's life?

God is our example—not our neighbors, the people we went to high school with, or our coworkers drowning in debt. God calls us, as Christians, to be different, to be set apart. That includes our finances. We are to act, speak, and spend differently than the world. When we obey His commands, we find fulfillment, contentment, and abundance in Him.

THE BLESSING OF BUDGETING MONEY

When we examine our financial habits and ensure that we're keeping money in the proper perspective, we're being good stewards of the financial gifts God has given us.

"How happy is the man who does not follow the advice of the wicked or take the path of sinners or join a group of mockers! Instead, his delight is in the LORD's instruction, and he meditates on it day and night. He is like a tree planted beside streams of water that bears its fruit in season and whose leaf does not wither. Whatever he does prospers" (Psalm 1:1-3).

Happiness in these verses expresses the joy and satisfaction found in trusting and being obedient to God.

When have you felt that kind of happiness?

Bottom line, what does money have to do w/ your relationship to Jesus?

How you spend your $ reveals your heart

Have you experienced that satisfaction with your finances? If not, what's holding you back?

The Bible is God's guide for showing us how to be good stewards of our wealth. If you can't remember anything else about this session, remember these two words: *perspective* and *principles*. Keep God's perspective about money. God sees money as resources given by Him for us to have lives that are full of joy and generosity. God knows that we can't do this on our own, so He has given us principles in His Word to help us live out His perspective on money.

THIS WEEK REFLECT ON . . .

> CLOSING QUESTIONS
• What financial legacy are you currently leaving? How does that compare with what you want to leave?
• What's your first step toward becoming a better money manager?
• Pinpoint two specific changes you'd like to make regarding the way you use your finances.

> GROWING WITH GOD
• Choose a verse that encourages you toward making the financial changes you've identified. Commit that verse to memory this week. Post it where you'll be regularly reminded to follow God's principles.
• Pray that God will help you maintain a biblical perspective on the gifts He's given you. Ask for guidance in the areas of struggle you've identified.

> MAKING A CHANGE
Money is personal. We don't like sharing our finances with just anyone. Yet we're not equipped to make all our money decisions without wise counsel. If God's calling you to make changes to your contributions, conservation, or consumption, seek out godly advice from someone who has been there, has a teacher's heart, and is willing to help you work through your struggles. Here are a couple places to start: Crown Financial Ministries (*crown.org*) and Dave Ramsey's Endorsed Local Providers (*daveramsey.com*).

Discerning
Our Days

The future is "something which everyone reaches at the rate of sixty minutes an hour, whatever he does, whoever he is."[1]
—C. S. Lewis, *The Screwtape Letters*

My (Micah's) youngest son played baseball for the first time this year. Once he had his glove, bat, and uniform, he was thrilled to play. He enjoyed learning the sport and hustled like I'd never seen before. But several kids had little interest in actually playing; they just wanted to draw pictures in the dirt. Recognizing this problem, the coach taught the team to be "baseball ready" on defense—meaning he wanted them to stay focused and keep their eyes on the batter, their gloves ready, and their posture active. If distractions abounded, the coach would yell, "Baseball ready!" and the kids knew what to do.

As Christians, we can live with a similar readiness. Living with a sense of urgency is a common motif in the Bible, particularly in the teachings of Jesus. He taught many parables about staying alert and being watchful— that is, living with keen focus and an active posture in obedience to God. Our lives can be evidence that we anticipate and are ready for Christ's return.

OTHER PARABLES
RELATED TO TIME
+ The Ten Virgins in
Matthew 25:1-13
+ The Fig Tree in
Mark 13:28-31

Revelation 21–22 gives a detailed description of what heaven and earth will be like after the second coming of Christ.

ON YOUR MARK

The Gospel of Luke emphasizes the importance of being ready for Christ's return. Jesus' parable of the faithful servant in Luke hits two important issues for our understanding of the stewardship of time:

Parable of the Faithful Servant

"Be ready for service and have your lamps lit. You must be like people waiting for their master to return from the wedding banquet so that when he comes and knocks, they can open the door for him at once. Those slaves the master will find alert when he comes will be blessed. I assure you: He will get ready, have them recline at the table, then come and serve them. If he comes in the middle of the night, or even near dawn, and finds them alert, those slaves are blessed. But know this: If the homeowner had known at what hour the thief was coming, he would not have let his house be broken into. You also be ready, because the Son of Man is coming at an hour that you do not expect."

First, it seems obvious that Jesus expects us to manage our time properly— and to do so with diligence and gladness. Jesus is coming back, and because we believe that truth, we should be alert and productive as we wait for Him. Just as a thief comes unexpectedly, how much more can the second coming of Christ catch us by surprise?

What does spending our time anxiously awaiting Christ's return look like—minute by minute, hour by hour?

> The three main themes from Luke 12 are **courageous confession** (vv. 1-12), **proper perspective** on possessions (vv. 13-34), and **faithful stewardship** (vv. 35-53).

Here's the remainder of the parable:

> "'Lord,' Peter asked, 'are You telling this parable to us or to everyone?' The Lord said: 'Who then is the faithful and sensible manager his master will put in charge of his household servants to give them their allotted food at the proper time? That slave whose master finds him working when he comes will be rewarded. I tell you the truth: He will put him in charge of all his possessions. But if that slave says in his heart, "My master is delaying his coming," and starts to beat the male and female slaves, and to eat and drink and get drunk, that slave's master will come on a day he does not expect him and at an hour he does not know. He will cut him to pieces and assign him a place with the unbelievers. And that slave who knew his master's will and didn't prepare himself or do it will be severely beaten. But the one who did not know and did things deserving of blows will be beaten lightly. Much will be required of everyone who has been given much. And even more will be expected of the one who has been entrusted with more'" (Luke 12:35-48).

The second issue regarding the stewardship of time from this passage is the essence of stewardship. Focus again on the last part of verse 48:

> "Much will be required of everyone who has been given much. And even more will be expected of the one who has been entrusted with more."

• ca. 45 B.C.: Julius Caesar introduced the 365-day year, with an extra day added every fourth year (Julian calendar)

• A.D. 525: Dionysius Exiguus creates a B.C. and A.D. calendar based on Jesus' birth

• A.D. 1582: Pope Gregory XIII reformed the Julian calendar creating the 354-day Gregorian calendar[2]

Up to this moment, how well have you utilized the time you've been given? What areas need more improvement?

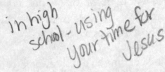

in high school - using your time for Jesus

JUGGLING WORK, LEISURE, AND MISSION

Growing up, my family (Micah's) had a roofing business called Carter & Sons Roofing. My granddad was the owner and mastermind, and my dad, uncles, and cousins all worked various jobs in the business. As a boy, I could make $25 to $50 a week, picking up shingles, nails, and other trash on a work site. That was big money. I have many fond memories of drowsy rides to a job site, climbing ladders, the smells of coffee and hot tar, and the sound of hammers pounding. For me, it was time well spent.

Read

We worked hard, but we played hard too. We took family vacations to theme parks, lakes, and state parks for camping and skiing and visiting friends. What's more, we served the Lord hard too. Not only was my granddad an entrepreneur, he was also a Baptist minister and church planter. Our family planted several churches on the West Coast. (I was born during a church plant in Arizona.) We evangelized, preached, sang, visited widows in nursing homes, and more—for the glory of Christ.

As a result of my upbringing, I believe it's possible to live a balanced life of work, leisure, and mission. I've seen it happen firsthand.

What examples have you seen of balancing career, family, personal time, and service to God?

or have you?

How have those examples shaped your decisions?

In Ephesians, the apostle Paul's letter encourages Christians to live with consistency and focus:

Read

> "Pay careful attention, then, to how you walk—not as unwise people but as wise—making the most of the time, because the days are evil. So don't be foolish, but understand what the Lord's will is" (Ephesians 5:15-17).

> Our use of time is not neutral; it can be evil if it is not invested for good. [3]

What distinguishes a wise person from an unwise one?

How do Paul's words impact you as you evaluate the way you spend your time?

Paul's instruction in these verses is both inspirational and convicting regarding his understanding of stewarding our time.

1. We are to be wise in how we walk—that is, how we live.
2. We are to make the most of the time we have, particularly because we live in dark days with distractions everywhere.
3. We are to understand what the will of the Lord is. It's not in foolishness, inattention, and wasting time.*

If we're being honest, living this out is challenging.

While we may desire to make the most of the time we have, we also fill our lives with nonessentials and allow ourselves to be distracted by things that don't cultivate a life of readiness and balance.

What things in your life do you currently balance well? What nonessentials need to be removed to better manage your time?

How to Understand God's Will

1. Discover what the Bible says about the answers you're looking for.
2. Seek counsel from wise Christians.
3. Pray for and eliminate answers that don't give God glory. [4]

---

* Facilitator: Spend time discussing the ways God's will is revealed to us. Be prepared to discuss how you've understood God's will in your own life. What role has spiritual disciplines played in seeking His will?

ESTABLISHING PRIORITIES

It's a common trend these days for people to develop their own bucket lists—you know, lists of stuff to accomplish before we kick the bucket. The assumption is we're so bogged down with work and other responsibilities that we don't have time to do the things we really want to do—like skydiving, visiting Thailand, finishing an Ironman Triathlon, or taking up photography. Unfortunately, as time passes, the more we realize how little time we have. James makes a great point comparing life to a vapor:

> "You don't even know what tomorrow will bring—what your life will be! For you are like smoke that appears for a little while, then vanishes. Instead, you should say, 'If the Lord wills, we will live and do this or that'" (James 4:14-15).

How often have you found yourself thinking, *I just don't have time,* or *I wish I had more time?* These statements are supported by an illusion: The items on our to-do lists aren't necessarily how God wants us to spend our time. We do, in fact, have enough time; we just don't use it properly or manage it effectively. We have enough time, every day, to do all that God has for us to do. Leland Ryken discusses this in *Redeeming the Time: A Christian Approach to Work and Leisure:*

> "If God is the one who allots us our time, we have a reason to conclude that we have sufficient time to do what God wants us to do. If our agendas are loaded beyond what we have time for, we are probably trying to do more than God expects or allows us to accomplish."[5]

So true

What do you consider to be your top three priorities right now?*

What stands in your way from having enough time to focus on these priorities?

---

* Facilitator: As a group, discuss what role prayer plays in establishing priorities and making decisions.

DON'T WORRY ABOUT A THING

This reality certainly doesn't mean prioritizing our time is going to come without difficulties. Two of the biggest hurdles for focusing on our priorities are stress and worry. Being overwhelmed with what's before you can weigh you down, limit your ability to make good decisions, and take away your joy. Yet God didn't design us to carry the burdens of what's to come.

When we worry about tomorrow, we begin to bear more than we were created to carry. God wants us to focus on Him as our ultimate priority because He is in control:

> "Look at the birds of the sky: They don't sow or reap or gather into barns, yet your heavenly Father feeds them. Aren't you worth more than they? Can any of you add a single cubit to his height by worrying? And why do you worry about clothes? Learn how the wildflowers of the field grow: they don't labor or spin thread. Yet I tell you that not even Solomon in all his splendor was adorned like one of these! If that's how God clothes the grass of the field, which is here today and thrown into the furnace tomorrow, won't He do much more for you—you of little faith? So don't worry, saying, 'What will we eat?' or 'What will we drink?' or 'What will we wear?' For the idolaters eagerly seek all these things, and your heavenly Father knows that you need them. But seek first the kingdom of God and His righteousness, and all these things will be provided for you. Therefore don't worry about tomorrow, because tomorrow will worry about itself. Each day has enough trouble of its own" (Matthew 6:26-34).

In what areas of life do you struggle with giving up control?

What hope do you find from knowing God will provide for you?

Facing the Valleys

As the lyrics to the hymn "Great Is Thy Faithfulness" express, when life becomes overwhelming, take refuge in God's mercies. They are new every day:

> "Because of the LORD's faithful loved we do not perish, for His mercies never end. They are new every morning; great is Your faithfulness! I say: The LORD is my portion, therefore I will put my hope in Him" (Lamentations 3:22-24).

---

* Facilitator: If you have Internet access, considering showing the North American Mission Board's video "Just a Thought." It's available at *vimeo.com/36898361*.

When you think about the past, present, or future, which one causes you the most concern? Why?

What could you give over to God that would help you change your view of the time you have on earth?

How we view what we're able to accomplish in a day can drastically influence how we evaluate our time. God is preparing us where we are right now for our tomorrow. When we surrender to His control over our lives today, we allow Him to equip us for tomorrow as well.

How does it change your worries and concerns when you view your life on a "today" basis? Does that add to or reduce your burden?

In the end, completing our bucket list is not critically important. As fun and exciting as that may be, what really matters is that we manage well this "vapor" of a life and view our time as valuable—entrusted to us by our Creator:

> **"Your eyes saw me when I was formless; all my days were written in Your book and planned before a single one of them began" (Psalm 139:16).**

How can we view our priorities in light of this verse?*

Psalm 31:15 reads, "The course of my life is in Your power . . ." Isn't that what James and Matthew were saying? From beginning to end, our lives are in the Lord's hands. And if He has entrusted the boundaries of our lives to us, how much more important is the use of our time?

Since such a large percentage of our life is spent working, it's important to have a healthy understanding of why our jobs matter.

---

* Facilitator: As a group, discuss how Psalm 139 makes you feel about yourself. Compare that feeling with your response to Jeremiah 1:5.

Work is for the glory of God. In the opening pages of the Bible, God placed Adam and Eve "in the garden of Eden to work it and watch over it" (Genesis 2:15). It wasn't until sin entered the picture that work became laborious, frustrating, and difficult (Genesis 3). So although we toil in our work now, when God restores all things in the new heavens and new earth, work will be redeemed as well.[6] After all, Jesus did say that if we were faithful with a little (that's stewardship), He would give us more responsibility in His kingdom, which implies and includes work.*

The Parable of the Talents

"Again, it will be like a man going on a journey, who called his servants and entrusted his property to them. To one he gave five talents of money, to another two talents, and to another one talent, each according to his ability. Then he went on his journey. The man who had received the five talents went at once and put his money to work and gained five more. So also, the one with the two talents gained two more. But the man who had received the one talent went off, dug a hole in the ground and hid his master's money.

After a long time the master of those servants returned and settled accounts with them. The man who had received the five talents brought the other five. 'Master,' he said, 'you entrusted me with five talents. See, I have gained five more.' His master replied, 'Well done, good and faithful servant! You have been faithful with a few things; I will put you in charge of many things. Come and share your master's happiness!' The man with the two talents also came. 'Master,' he said, 'you entrusted me with two talents; see, I have gained two more.' His master replied, 'Well done, good and faithful servant! You have been faithful with a few things; I will put you in charge of many things. Come and share your master's happiness!' Then the man who had received the one talent came. 'Master,' he said, 'I knew that you are a hard man, harvesting where you have not sown and gathering where you have not scattered seed. So I was afraid and went out and hid your talent in the ground. See, here is what belongs to you.' His master replied, 'You wicked, lazy servant! So you knew that I harvest where I have not sown and gather where I have

"I'm concerned that too many of us have a savings mindset; we want to keep what we have. We're playing not to lose. But the parable of the talents is all about an investment mindset—risking what you have to get more. It's playing to win."[7]
—Mark Batterson, *Chase the Lion*

---

* Facilitator: For more background on responsibility in God's kingdom, read the blog post "When We All Get to Heaven?" (July 17, 2008) by Russell Moore, available at *russellmoore.com*.

The man on the long journey in this parable symbolizes Jesus and the lengthy delay that will precede His second coming.

One talent was the ancient equivalent of 20 years of a day-laborer's salary—or $576,000 in today's terms.[8]

not scattered seed? Well then, you should have put my money on deposit with the bankers, so that when I returned I would have received it back with interest. Take the talent from him and give it to the one who has the ten talents. For everyone who has will be given more, and he will have an abundance. Whoever does not have, even what he has will be taken from him. And throw that worthless servant outside, into the darkness, where there will be weeping and gnashing of teeth.'" (Matthew 25:14-30, NIV).

What struck you from this passage regarding the use of time?

How can this parable help shape your approach to work?*

What risks are you willing to take with the time God has given you?

Verses on Idolatry
Exodus 20:4-5; 32
Numbers 21
2 Kings 17:7-8,33; 18:4
Joshua 24:14
Isaiah 44:9-20
Colossians 3:5

AMERICAN IDOLS

The reality is, how we use our time exposes idolatry in our hearts. Work and leisure are both susceptible to this idolatry. If we put in 50-plus hours a week in the office and then work 20-plus hours at home, chances are, life is off-balance and other priorities suffer. Bottom line: Workaholism is sinful and destructive. Idolatry is subtle here, because it's likely that workaholics find their value and worth in their work (and not in Christ). There's great value in working diligently, as we should do. But as Christians, our career focus should be less about climbing the corporate ladder and more about how we can honor Christ through our work.

---

* Facilitator: Using the Parable of the Talents, define *faithfulness*. If time allows, discuss what faithfulness with our time looks like on a daily basis. What does it look like long-term?

Paul left a great example of this in the Book of Acts, as he worked to establish the Corinthian church:

> "After this, he left Athens and went to Corinth, where he found a Jewish man named Aquila, a native of Pontus, who had recently come from Italy with his wife Priscilla because Claudius had ordered all the Jews to leave Rome. Paul came to them, and being of the same occupation, stayed with them and worked, for they were tentmakers by trade. He reasoned in the synagogue every Sabbath and tried to persuade both Jews and Greeks" (Acts 18:1-4).

How can you determine whether your focus is on a healthy work ethic or if it has become idolatry?

There are two good points of measure to evaluate idolizing a career. First, determine how much time you spend thinking about work (checking e-mails, worrying about deadlines, etc.) when you're not actually working. And secondly, consider how much time you spend with God (praying, reading His Word, etc.) on a daily or weekly basis. If you don't have time to make God a priority, something is out of alignment.

Evaluate your career goals. What changes need to be made regarding the hours you work and how your work affects life at home and with God?

"Remember to dedicate the Sabbath day . . ."

There may be nothing else quite as neglected in our lives today as *Sabbath*. In a country that prizes busyness and productivity, the idea of *stopping* is useless. Maybe that is part of the mystery of Sabbath. The noun means an intermission; the verb means to cease and desist, to stop. But the true beauty of Sabbath is not just in the rest that happens when we stop—it's in the reflection that is meant to take place during that rest.

God was the first one to introduce this practice, and He did so not because He was tired; He stopped because He wanted to reflect and celebrate what He had accomplished. This coming Sabbath day, don't plan out your week. Don't go to the movies. Don't pay your bills. Rather, follow the Lord's example and reflect. Reflect on what the Lord has taught you this week. Journal about your experiences. Don't concern yourself with the challenges of tomorrow, but cease and enjoy the work of God in your life over the past several days.[9]

We can also infer the reverse of work idolatry: If we drop hours and hours into entertainment, hobbies, recreation, and leisure—and these become our consuming passion—chances are, our life focus is off-balance.

IT'S ALL FUN AND GAMES, OR IS IT?

Hedonism is the idea that pleasure or happiness is the highest good and main goal of life. Let's cut to the chase: The sole pursuit of pleasure is sinful and destructive. Idolatry is subtle here too, because it's good to have recreation and happiness; but pleasure is a stingy god, unlike Christ, in whom is our true rest and satisfaction.

In which area are you more likely to struggle—workaholism or hedonism? Why?

A 2010 report from the Bureau of Labor Statistics found that Americans, age 15 and older, spent an average of five hours a day on leisure activities—including TV, socializing, reading, sports and exercise, gaming, and so forth.[10] The same study revealed that Americans spend more than half of their leisure time watching television.[11]

God gave us skills and passions—and even the necessity of work and rest. So these things in and of themselves are not ungodly uses of time. It's within the extreme focus and subsequent neglect of other priorities that we run into problems. It's important to keep our free time in balance—especially since mission is likely the first thing to slack off when work or leisure dominate.

How do you know when you're correctly balancing time for you and time for service to others?

As followers of Christ, our mission is to make disciples of all nations (Matthew 28:19-20) and also, as James puts it, living out true religion looks like this:

> **"Pure and undefiled religion before our God and Father is this: to look after orphans and widows in their distress and to keep oneself unstained by the world" (James 1:27).**

We cannot spend so much time and effort on entertainment if it means we neglect our responsibilities as Christians to love God and love others. We have kingdom business to attend to, but it often gets shuffled aside for work, recreation, and other commitments.

How can work and leisure be channels that facilitate mission?*

> An average of 3.5 percent of men and 4.6 percent of women, age 25-34, volunteered on any given day from 2006-2010.[12]

Go back to the apostle Paul in Acts 18. As a church-planting missionary, he invested a year and a half of ministry in Corinth. The believers at Corinth formed a local church, and Paul enjoyed "teaching the word of God among them" (Acts 18:11). He merged work, mission, and fulfillment.

Practically speaking, how can we get everything done and still first focus on our obedience to God?

ALL TIME IS HOLY

We often perceive non-ministry related jobs as "secular" work and ministry-related jobs as "sacred" work. Many think what pastors and missionaries do with their time is holy and sacred, but what CPAs, dentists, students, and stay-at-home moms do with their time is secular. John Piper, in *Don't Waste Your Life,* is right: We must understand "secular" not as bad or irrelevant, but as strategic for God's glory.[13]

secular vs. sacred jobs

If your work is not specifically ministry-related, how does this notion affect your perception of your work time?

realize my mission field is huge

---

* Facilitator: Take a few minutes to tell a story about obedience to God from your life. How did you find fulfillment and joy from participating in God's mission?

Leland Ryken, in his book *Redeeming the Time,* is again helpful:

> "Solving the problem of time begins by acknowledging that time is not our possession. It is a gift from God. We are simply allowed to use it as stewards to whom it has been entrusted. While this acknowledgment does not solve the problems surrounding the *quantity* of time at our disposal, it instills an attitude toward time that can make us value the *quality* of the time that God has given us as a gift. If time is holy, then the work and leisure with which we fill it are also holy."[14]

What evidence supports that all time is holy?

We must apply the education, passions, gifts, skills, and callings that we have to our careers—wherever we work. Let's remove the wall between what we perceive to be sacred and to be secular. Once we collapse the wall, we'll see the time spent working (and in leisure) as vitally important for how we glorify God and fulfill His design for us. In addition, we find a growing sense of enjoyment and responsibility in using our time for God's glory.

Effectively Managing Time

Evaluate the necessities.

Consider the legacy you'll leave.

Establish practical goals.

Break tasks into small steps.

Quit procrastinating.

Reward your accomplishments.

There's a tremendous example of this idea in Exodus 35–36. When Moses instructed the Israelites to build the tabernacle (by God's command), he made an appeal not only for the people to provide the materials, but also for "skilled craftsmen" to "come and make everything that the LORD has commanded" (Exodus 35:10). Men and women, whose hearts were moved to serve and contribute, did so "by virtue of their skill" (v. 26).

What's even more fascinating, Moses calls out two men by name—Bezalel and Oholiab—for their abilities and the importance of having them apply themselves and their skills. Here's the full account:

"Moses then said to the Israelites: 'Look, the LORD has appointed by name Bezalel son of Uri, son of Hur, of the tribe of Judah. He has filled him with God's Spirit, with wisdom, understanding, and ability in every kind of craft to design artistic works in gold, silver, and bronze, to cut gemstones for mounting, and to carve wood for work in every kind of artistic craft. He has also given both him and Oholiab son of Ahisamach, of the tribe of Dan, the ability to teach others. He has filled them with skill to do all the work of a gem cutter; a designer; an embroiderer in blue, purple, and scarlet yarn and fine linen; and a weaver. They can do every kind of craft and design artistic designs.

. . . .

Bezalel, Oholiab, and all the skilled people are to work based on everything the Lord has commanded. The Lord has given them wisdom and understanding to know how to do all the work of constructing the sanctuary" (Exodus 35:30–36:1).

> "It is not what a man does that determines whether his work is sacred or secular, it is why he does it."[15]
> —A. W. Tozer,
> *The Pursuit of God*

Notice a few of things here:

1. The Lord appointed them to do this kind of work. It wasn't by chance that these guys became proficient in their skill set. God created them and directed them for those abilities (see Psalm 139:16 and Philippians 2:13).

2. God filled them with wisdom and understanding to do their work. These folks were skilled beyond their own efforts: God placed within them the understanding of their work that made them excel.

3. These men were renown for their skills. Becoming an expert or an all-star involves putting in hard work, practice, and determination. Professional athletes have natural, physical abilities for sure, but they've also dedicated a lifetime to their sport and put in countless hours of practice and preparation to succeed. The same goes for these skilled craftsmen; they put in the time applying themselves to their natural crafts, and it paid off. They were singled out to glorify God in a specific way:

> "Do you see a man skilled in his work? He will stand in the presence of kings. He will not stand in the presence of unknown men" (Proverbs 22:29).

List your God-given gifts and abilities. What does it mean to you that God gave you those passions/skills for a specific reason?*

CREATING MARGIN

Because we live in a time-crunched society, any time spent without immediate results seems wasteful. And if we're not careful, we'll neglect the need for personal margin.

[handwritten: God rested & We should too]

Often we become so preoccupied with what must get done and how much time we have left that we forget to care for ourselves. Our bodies are not equipped for continuous activity. We need rest and room for reflection. Additionally, we must leave breathing room for God-given opportunities the Lord brings our way.

Jesus left a great example of this in the Gospel of Mark. After feeding the 5,000, the apostles were eager to tell Jesus of all they had accomplished, but He refocused them:

> "Life is a journey, but it is not a race. Do yourself a favor and slow down."[16]
> —Richard Swenson, *Margin*

> "The apostles gathered around Jesus and reported to Him all that they had done and taught. He said to them, 'Come away by yourselves to a remote place and rest for a while.' For many people were coming and going, and they did not even have time to eat" (Mark 6:30-31).

[handwritten: Spring Break is a great chance]

When have you been so focused on the task at hand that you've forgotten to care for yourself? What were the results?

It's in the margin—the down time—that we allow ourselves to rest, reflect, refuel, and reaffirm how God wants us to spend our lives. Richard Swenson, author of *Margin: Restoring Emotional, Physical, Financial, and Time Reserves to Overloaded Lives* argues,

> "Margin exists for the needs of the kingdom, for the service of one another, for the building of community. It exists, just as we exist, for the purpose of being available to God."[17]

---

* Facilitator: If it seems appropriate, go around the room and share what talents and abilities you appreciate in each of your group members. Give others time to participate as well.

Can you think of a time when you had a well-balanced margin in your life? What effect did it have?

What changes can you make to create margin in your life?

Psalm 90 provides a powerful wrap-up of our discussion on the stewardship of time. These verses remind us of the brevity of life:

> "Our lives last seventy years or, if we are strong, eighty years. Even the best of them are struggle and sorrow; indeed, they pass quickly and we fly away. . . . Teach us to number our days carefully so that we may develop wisdom in our hearts (vv. 10-12)."

There are blessings found in making the most of our time, for in doing so, we gain wisdom and joy. Life moves past us quickly, so use your time well.

watch video then do closing

THIS WEEK REFLECT ON . . .

> CLOSING QUESTIONS
• How do you want to be remembered in light of the fact that life is short?
• How would you describe the balance of work, leisure, and mission in your life? What specific ways can you adjust and better manage this balance?

> MAKING A CHANGE
Take a day for a "Sabbath"-like rest and reflection. Unplug and deviate from the normal routine to spend time with God or serve others.

> GROWING WITH GOD
Reflect on Luke 12:48. Ask God to open your eyes to all He's entrusted to you—giftings, work, passions, and so forth—and how you should care for those things.

"When you are given much, much is required."

When we take a hard look at the way we spend our days, sometimes that compels us to make a drastic change. For one young adult's journey to Christ's call on her life, watch "Sara's Story" at *vimeo.com/17998361.*

Building Healthy Relationships

"Man is a knot into which relationships are tied."[1]
—Antoine de Saint-Exupéry,
Flight to Arras

One of the first things God did after creating Adam was express that it wasn't good for Adam to be alone (Genesis 2:18). So God gave Adam a partner, Eve. Yes, their relationship gives us the biblical foundation for marriage, but it was also the catalyst for all future relationships. None of our relationships—with parents, siblings, neighbors, friends, roommates, coworkers, extended family, and so on—would exist if God hadn't noticed the need for Adam to have someone to share his life with.[2]

We need each other. We were created for community. Yet our relationships don't always come easily or naturally. They take effort, intentionality, and "attentionality"—pursuing interaction and avoiding neglect. Let's consider how we can enhance our relationships with Christ and others.

handwritten margin note: What rel. matter? - God, what? - others order?

THE ONE TRUE RELATIONSHIP
Read Mark 12:28-30:

HEBREWS 12:29 says that "our God is a consuming fire." Where else have we seen Him burning?
+ Exodus 3: God's presence in the burning bush.
+ Exodus 13:21: God leads Israel through wilderness as a cloud by day and fire by night.
+ 1 Kings 18:38: God consumes Elijah's waterlogged altar in a blaze of glory.
Where is God burning in your life? What is He burning away? What is He raising from the ashes?

"One of the scribes approached. When he heard them debating and saw that Jesus answered them well, he asked Him, 'Which command is the most important of all?' 'This is the most important,' Jesus answered: 'Listen, Israel! The Lord our God, the Lord is One. Love the Lord your God with all your heart, with all your soul, with all your mind, and with all your strength.'"

God is not requesting a Facebook-like friendship. He doesn't want occasional status updates. God says He wants everything. Reread the passage in Mark: The word "love" implies affection and attention. Then you see "heart," "soul," and "mind." God doesn't mince words: He wants total access. Every. Part. Of. You.

How does it feel to know God wants a highly intense, honest, consuming relationship with you? Does it sound frightening or exciting?

Have you ever had a relationship with someone who loved you completely, wanted the absolute best for you, and already knew all your faults and dreams? How did that relationship change your approach to life?

What makes a total access relationship with God difficult?

discuss

How much free time per day do you spend online? How much time do you spend connecting with Jesus? How would your relationship with Him change if you spent more time praying and less time online?

DRAWING CLOSE TO GOD THROUGH SPIRITUAL DISCIPLINES

A deep, engaging relationship with God comes when we make an intentional effort to become more Christlike. Spiritual transformation is not automatic. Spiritual disciplines are those things we do that grow our relationship with God and make us more like Christ.

what does discipline mean? - spiritual discipline?

7 STEPS TO SPIRITUAL GROWTH

Without regular attention, our relationship with God will become stagnant or wither completely. Here's a strategy for personal spiritual growth.

1. Make growth a priority.
Set a specific time and develop a specific plan for spending time with God.

2. Set personal goals.
Set goals and write them down. Place them where you can be reminded of them periodically.

3. Identify key resources.
Certainly your Bible and devotional materials are important. Sometimes a key resource is another person with whom you can share your thoughts, feelings, and discoveries.

4. Develop accountability groups.
Informal or formal accountability groups can motivate us to follow through on our commitments.

5. Model growth for others.
Share with others what you've discovered, particularly when you have a remarkable spiritual insight.

6. Evaluate periodically.
Check regularly that you're progressing toward your goals and make adjustments as necessary.

7. Mentor others.
Enlist someone to be your spiritual apprentice and invest yourself in another person with whom you can share your spiritual pilgrimage. Mentoring others is how Jesus invested Himself in His followers.[3]

Before you equate "discipline" with "dullness," take a look at the benefits that come standard with the spiritual disciplines package: insight and intimacy with the God who wants all of you to know all of Him. Once you get into the groove of spiritual disciplines, you'll be tracking with King David, who confessed,

> **"As a deer longs for streams of water, so I long for You, God"**
> **(Psalm 42:1).**

Let's get longing. How? Spiritual disciplines promote a routine that keeps your mind, heart, and soul centered on the Lord.

Though there isn't a specific list of disciplines in the Bible, some can be gleaned from various passages. Dallas Willard, in *The Spirit of the Disciplines*, compiles a list to start with, separating them into two categories: disciplines of abstinence and of engagement.[4]

PURITANS: SPIRITUAL DISCIPLINES ARE FOR REVELING IN GOD

Not as straitlaced as they've been portrayed, Puritans were passionate about pursuing intimacy with Jesus.

Isaac Ambrose, a 17th-century Puritan pastor, cautioned against legalism in spiritual disciplines ("[they] cannot save, but they let the soul in to Christ.") Ambrose and other Puritans esteemed the disciplines (or "secret duties") for their access to Jesus' presence, promoting them for the "sweet refreshment" found within them.[5]

Disciplines of abstinence include:
- solitude (alone with God)
- silence (quiet with God)
- fasting (from food and/or the distraction of media)
- frugality
- chastity
- secrecy (discovering God's secrets)
- sacrifice

Disciplines of engagement include:
- study
- worship
- celebration
- service
- prayer
- fellowship
- confession (to God and to others who will encourage and support us)
- submission (saying no to pride)

Which area could you do better to increase intimacy w/Jesus?

---

* **Facilitator:** Spend some time discussing spiritual disciplines that the group could try out this week. For more depth, consider reading Donald Whitney's *Spiritual Disciplines for the Christian Life*.

SESSION THREE MANAGE

Consider the list of abstinence and engagement disciplines. What have you practiced in the past? How did those disciplines affect your relationship with God?

WAYS TO PRACTICE THE DISCIPLINES

1. Go for a solo walk/hike, clocking some solitude and silence with Him.

2. Log on to *mystudybible.com* and search "secrets." See also Deuteronomy 29:29. Why would God want to keep secrets?

3. Volunteer to serve. Search "homeless shelters" and your city to find opportunities near you.

Pick three of each to try this week. How did it go? What did you observe?

Beware the legalism that can creep in when practicing the disciplines, remembering that observing them does not earn you points with God and failing to observe them does not lose points with God.

What can we gain from practicing spiritual disciplines?

LEGALISM
Trying to attain or maintain rightness (righteousness) with God by human effort. Working to maintain salvation rather than resting in grace.[6]

Again, practicing the disciplines is not about earning points and changing your outward behavior (though it will change). The purpose of practicing the disciplines is found in Galatians 4:19: that "Christ is formed within you." Not that your behavior gets better, but that your will and heart are changed to be more like Christ's. You exchange your "heart of stone" (hardened by sin and by rules) for a "heart of [His] flesh" (Ezekiel 36:26), governed by His passions and His appetites.

Read John 15:5:

> "I am the vine; you are the branches. The one who remains in Me and I in him produces much fruit, because you can do nothing without Me."

How can the heart be changed? What part do you play in the process? What's the Spirit's role?

MANAGING RELATIONSHIPS WITH OTHERS
Read Mark 12:31:

"The second is: Love your neighbor as yourself. There is no other command greater than these."

Jesus transitions from talking about the vertical relationship we have with God to the horizontal relationship with people. These two commands constitute the SparkNotes of Scripture. And both are tricky to carry out; hence the helpful hint in John 15:5 to remain in Christ. On our own, we're utterly powerless to do what's best for us, no matter what our well-intentioned willpower tells us.

Our sinful nature longs for us to think about ourselves—mainly how to please self. This command (love neighbor as self) tells us to think about ourselves for the purpose of research: to discover how to treat others well.

> "We justify the evil we do to our brother [when] he is merely an adversary, an accused. To restore communication, to see . . . his integrity, his worthiness of love, we have to see ourselves as similarly accused along with him . . . and needing, with him, the ineffable gift of grace and mercy to be saved. Then, instead of pushing him down, trying to climb out by using his head as a stepping-stone for ourselves, we help ourselves to rise by helping him to rise."[7]
>
> —Thomas Merton,
> *The Hidden Ground of Love*

Our happiness blocks our obedience to this command. It doesn't delight us to love some people as we love ourselves. They honestly don't deserve it. And they certainly haven't loved us as they've loved themselves. True, but chew on another fact: "While we were still sinners, Christ died for us!" Just when you think you've got some obstinate ground to stand on, Romans 5:8 delivers the smackdown.

If you truly considered how to love your neighbor as yourself, what would you change about how you treat the ones closest to you?

---

* Facilitator: Ask people in your group to think of someone they struggle to "love as themselves." Ask them to consider what exactly repulses them about that person, and if they can find any of that trait in themselves as well.

SESSION THREE MANAGE

CLARIFYING EXPECTATIONS

How can we love our neighbors better? By clarifying expectations. Most relationships experience hardship from unmet expectations.

When I (Chip) got married a couple of years ago, I thought our union would just work out—no expectation-setting needed. This regrettable insight led to most of the conflicts we faced in the beginning.

The fact is, my wife (Chip's) was raised in a family structure unfamiliar to me, just as I was raised in one unfamiliar to her. Our uncommunicated expectations from different family backgrounds wreaked havoc on us early on.

As Christians, we focus on the obvious expectations: to be nice, be caring, be respectful, don't cheat, don't be abusive, and so forth. And these generalities are all well and good. But to give love as you would want to be loved needs specifics.

Spend some time reflecting on what words help others feel loved, valued, and respected. What actions make them feel loved? Are you listening to their answers or just ruminating on your own?

✴ Now turn your focus on God: What makes Him feel loved?

How does loving others
show God love?
- obeying commands He has
given mark 12
- whatever you do for
the least of there..

Thankfully, God's already inscribed His trigger points for love in Scripture. God wants us to:

- Follow the Ten Commandments (Exodus 20:1-17)
- Thank Him for His love (Psalm 136:26)
- Seek Him diligently (Proverbs 8:17)
- Be merciful to others (Matthew 9:13)
- Love others as He first loved us (John 13:34-35)
- Give over our anxieties to Him (1 Peter 5:6-7).

Recall from Mark 12:29-31 God's specific expectation inherent in the order of love priorities: Love God first, then others as yourself. God desires a relationship with us that supersedes any other in our lives. Again, He wants a total committed love from us—one that encompasses our whole heart, soul, and mind.

When we're that sold-out for God, we seek fulfillment through our relationship with Him rather than the closest people in our lives. It's a great system of priority, because we don't know how to love others unless we're totally in love with God.

This sequence of preference is also a safeguard for us. When we seek fulfillment through relationships with our spouse, children, parents, friends, and coworkers first, then we focus life on their happiness above all else—something we cannot control or guarantee. Giving them precedence also hinders our response to Jesus' daily call and opportunities for us. If He makes a request of you that might disturb the convenience of family and friends, you'll cater to their desires instead of His good work.

✗ Who are you putting first on your love list? Why?

Who would people around you say you love? - God -self -boys - technology - unsure of what / who you love

What expectations of love does God have for you?

_____

What expectations do your friends have for you?

GETTING SERIOUS ABOUT PRIORITIES
Read Luke 9:57-62:

"As they were traveling on the road someone said to Him, 'I will follow You wherever You go!' Jesus told him, 'Foxes have dens, and birds of the sky have nests, but the Son of Man has no place to lay His head.' Then He said to another, 'Follow Me.' 'Lord,' he said, 'first let me go bury my father.' But He told him, 'Let the dead bury their own dead, but you go and spread the news of the kingdom of God.' Another also said, 'I will follow You, Lord, but first let me go and say good-bye to those at my house.' But Jesus said to him, 'No one who puts his hand to the plow and looks back is fit for the kingdom of God.'"

Also read Luke 14:25-27:

"Now great crowds were traveling with Him. So He turned and said to them: 'If anyone comes to Me and does not hate his own father and mother, wife and children, brothers and sisters—yes, and even his own life—he cannot be My disciple. Whoever does not bear his own cross and come after Me cannot be My disciple.'"

How do these passages strike you? Is Jesus being insensitive to family values? Explain.

_____

He communicates that Christ must come first before everyone and everything in our lives. Even our families must not come before our relationship with Christ. Yet Jesus doesn't want us to treat our families as second-class citizens. Scripture instructs us to take care of our spouses and children. We're called to care for those God has entrusted to us:

> **"But if anyone does not provide for his own, that is his own household, he has denied the faith and is worse than an unbeliever" (1 Timothy 5:8).**

However, to follow Jesus means to let Him have total access to our lives. Even Mary had moments of confusion about what her Son was doing. She wanted what was best for Him, but He was focused on fulfilling the mission He received from His Heavenly Father.

Has God nudged you to do something that didn't coincide with your parents' agenda? What did you do? How did it make you feel?

As previously mentioned, your relationship with Christ is the key to every other relationship you have. His love works in you and through you to shape you into the friend, coworker, child, spouse, parent, or neighbor that you could never be without a solid relationship with Him. If Christ comes first, that will dictate how others are treated. You can't treat others well if you're disconnected from Him.

Have you noticed times when your relationships suffered while you were out of touch with Jesus? Have you seen improvements in other relationships when you felt the closest to Jesus?

---

* Facilitator: Ask group members if they have a relationship that lets them be imperfect. Ask them how they respond when someone lets them down in a relationship. How do they repair the relationship?

LET GO OF RELATIONSHIP PERFECTION

To enjoy the relationships we're given, keep in mind a nugget of wisdom: Relationships aren't perfect. There are no cookie-cutter solutions for every problem that pops up. Relationships are delightful, fulfilling, stretching, draining, encouraging, and challenging. There will always be something in our relationship with God and with people that will require growth and improvement. Maturity in our relationships is a process that will never cease until we see Jesus face-to-face.

In fact, a healthy relationship is a repairing relationship. We all make mistakes. We all need grace. The main goal is to keep our priorities straight: Christ first; others second.

Consider how you're presenting yourself in current relationships—in person and online. Do you present your most winning front, offering humorous insights or event recaps while never letting your real, imperfect self show? Give examples.

How do you feel when you make a mistake in your relationships? How would you like to feel?

How do you treat others when they make a mistake? How would you like them to feel?

REAL RELATIONSHIPS

If you're offering nothing but a well-crafted, inauthentic self to others, you'll reap what you sow: inauthentic relationships, not letting anyone (least of all you) get to know the real person within.

What do you need to allow to surface—opinions, conflict, imperfections—to let real relationships grow? How can you let you be you while showing respect to yourself, God, and others?

List of People with Whom I Can Be Myself:

-
-
-
-
-

In which relationships can you make a mistake? Which ones don't allow you to mess up? What can you do to allow your real self (with imperfections) to show up?

Our society yearns for connections. That's why Facebook, Twitter, Pinterest, and Instagram are so popular. We want to be connected, no matter how superficially. If you want more meaningful relationships, allow Christ to work deeply in your heart. His work helps us find new depth and new life.

How can a relationship with Christ deepen other relationships?

How many Facebook friends do you have? Compare that number with how many people you'd call if disaster struck you (parent died, divorce occurred, job lost, etc.).

HOW TO SNAG A MENTOR/DISCIPLE

1. Pray. Ask God to bring mentor/disciple candidates into your life and clue you in to them.

2. Approach them. Ask if they're interested in trying out this role to see how it goes.

3. Make plans. Set up meetings and discuss what you'd both like out of the situation. Then follow through.

PURSUING TEACHABLE RELATIONSHIPS: MENTORING AND DISCIPLESHIP*

Why did Jesus pour time, care, and teachings into 12 ordinary men? He needed to reach the world, but He spent the most of His time with those 12 guys. Jesus walked with them, ate with them, and did ministry with them. He took advantage of many teachable moments, pointing out the kingdom of God, explaining the secrets that were about to unfold.

---

* Facilitator: As a group, define *mentoring* and *discipling*. Discuss biblical people who exemplified these kinds of relationships, like Paul and Timothy.

SESSION THREE MANAGE

After Christ died, resurrected, reappeared, and ascended, the gospel message was left in the hands of these 12 men who impacted the world.

Why did Jesus spend His precious time with the 12?

Mentoring and discipleship are the most efficient ways for Christians to mature in their faith, providing the earthly accountability and guidance believers need to grow. We need the equipping and encouragement of mentors and disciples in our lives. We need to not only be mentored and discipled, but to mentor and disciple someone else.

Mentors Offer:
• wisdom
• technical knowledge
• assistance
• support
• empathy
• respect

Is there someone you would consider as a possible mentor? How might you approach them about establishing a mentor relationship?

Who could you begin to disciple? What affect could your knowledge and experience have on that person's life?

The word "training" in Greek is *gymnasia*. Picture your spiritual training room as a gym. What equipment would you like to try out: the mentoring rings, the solitude beam, the sacrifice bars, the fellowship weights? Who is your Trainer? How often will you come to the gym to get toned?

IT'S ALL ABOUT THE TRAINING

Mentoring and discipling train your mind and spirit as the spiritual disciplines do, building your relationship with God (loving Him with all your heart, mind, and soul) and your mentor/disciple (your neighbor).

Speaking of getting in mental shape, let's read 1 Timothy 4:8:

"The training of the body has a limited benefit, but godliness is beneficial in every way, since it holds promise for the present life and also for the life to come."

What activities fill your day? Which of them are "beneficial in every way . . . for the present life and also for the life to come"?

We live in a health-conscious society. People are eager to get fit or at least appear fit. Check your true desire: Do you want to be spiritually fit or appear spiritually fit?

When we aren't connected to the Vine (John 15), we tend to lose our desire to be fit or transfer it to a desire to appear fit—neither of which has an eternal benefit.

When we do choose spiritual training, we're also choosing patience: The rewards of spiritual health and wellness won't be immediately evident. Just as biceps don't bulge after one pull-up, spiritual fitness will not show instantly. You'll need training and practice—being in the midst of temptation, conflict, or distraction and choosing to turn to Him—to see results. And anyway, the results are best left to your Trainer; He sees your improvements and imperfections and loves you no matter your skill. Your job is just to show up for training—and even that takes a nudge from the Spirit.

What spiritual training are you excited about? What are you scared of? What seems like a tedious exercise?

THIS WEEK REFLECT ON . . .

> MAKING A CHANGE

Spend some time this week reviewing what you learned in this session and working through the following questions. Use the notes pages provided to jot down your thoughts.

1. Growing with God

- Do you understand the intensity of love God has for you? What evidence supports your answer?
- How do you respond to God's intense, consuming love?
- What kind of person could you be if you lived in the awareness of God's love for you?

2. Growing with Others

- Are you fully showing up in your relationship with others or just offering a part of your true self?
- What keeps you from showing up? What do you fear?
- Do you know how to show up and show respect to yourself and others in the process?

3. Taking the Next Step   *find new ways to love/serve God*

- What actions might you take to remind yourself of God's passion for you?
- How can you encourage yourself to be fully you (imperfections and all) in your relationships with coworkers, neighbors, roommates, friends, significant others, and family members?

> CLOSING THOUGHTS

- Choose three spiritual disciplines to incorporate in your daily schedule this week. Record how you feel during and after your training.
- Reflect on recent decisions you've made and how often you've allowed other people's expectations of you to overtake God's desires for you.
- Pray about the need to have a mentor in your Christian walk and to disciple someone else. Consider working through *Mentor: How Along-the-Way Discipleship Will Change Your Life* by Chuck Lawless (available for purchase at *threadsmedia.com*) as your next Bible study. It further examines our desire for deep, meaningful connection with others and how that impacts our spiritual walk.

Ruling the
Earth

"If creation has suffered the
consequences of human sin,
it will also enjoy the fruits of
human deliverance."[1]
　　—Douglas J. Moo in *Keeping God's Earth*

When I (Micah) was about 9 years old, some friends and I found a beautiful goose while wading in a creek. As mischievous boys, instead of admiring its majesty, we decided to provoke it by throwing rocks at it. That angry, bloody goose chased us out of the creek! Although I didn't let on to my friends how I felt, I remember feeling remorse for my actions. I don't know if that goose lived or died that day, and I've always regretted doing such a mean thing to that innocent creature. Part of that regret is because I know God has called humanity to relate differently to creation.

In this session, we're going to discuss what it means to be good stewards of God's creation, noting biblical and practical ideas related to creation care to better understand our role as managers of the earth He has entrusted to us.

WHY SHOULD CREATION CARE MATTER?

Biblically speaking, our environment is part of God's creation. Just as we're called to care for widows and orphans (James 1:27), we're called to watch over the earth. Let's look at a few verses to better understand why caring for the earth matters.

In Genesis 1, we find God's design for creation: Humanity is His representative on earth.

HEBREW MEANINGS
- To rule = *radah*.
- To subdue = *kabash*. May also be translated "to bring into bondage."
- To work = *abad*. May also be translated "to serve."
- To watch over = *shamar*. May also be translated "to guard, preserve, care for."

"Then God said, 'Let Us make man in Our image, according to Our likeness. They will rule the fish of the sea, the birds of the sky, the livestock, all the earth, and the creatures that crawl on the earth.' So God created man in His own image; He created him in the image of God; He created them male and female. God blessed them, and God said to them, 'Be fruitful, multiply, fill the earth, and subdue it. Rule the fish of the sea, the birds of the sky, and every creature that crawls on the earth'" (vv. 26-28).*

What strikes you about God's intention for humanity relating to creation?

---

* Facilitator: Read John 1:1-3 and Colossians 1:15-20. How do these verses affect your perception of Genesis 1:26-28? What's Christ's role in creation? How do all these verses help you appreciate the work of Christ in our world?

In Colossians, it's revealed that all of creation belongs to Jesus—all the animals, plants, minerals, waters, and so forth:

> "For everything was created by Him, in heaven and on earth, the visible and the invisible, whether thrones or dominions or rulers or authorities—all things have been created through Him and for Him" (Colossians 1:16).

God created the world, and it all belongs to Him. And when Jesus Himself was asked which command was the greatest, He said:

> "Love the Lord your God with all your heart, with all your soul, and with all your mind. This is the greatest and most important command. The second is like it: Love your neighbor as yourself" (Matthew 22:37-39).

Confused by the scientific data for environmental issues, or tired of the political debates around global warming or alternative energy? Nonetheless, our obligation remains the same: to love our neighbors as ourselves and to fulfill God's intention for us as managers of creation. We may disagree on some points, but we can agree to focus on ways to consume less, conserve more, and contribute for the love of our neighbors.

How can we be obedient to Christ's command to love Him if we don't care for His creation?

How can we love our neighbors if we don't care for the very air they breathe, the food they eat, and the land on which they live?

UNDERSTANDING OUR ROLE

Being created in God's image and likeness, humans have the responsibility to "rule" all living creatures and to "subdue" the earth. Adam was "mayor" of the garden-city where God placed him. Genesis 2:8 says,

> "The Lord God planted a garden in Eden, in the east, and there He placed the man He had formed."

He was to do more than just plow the soil. He was responsible for a robust environment of animals, trees, rivers, and more. Adam was to care for, watch over, and carry on the creation that God had given to him. And that servant responsibility passes down to each generation.

Theologians have referred to our responsibility to rule and to subdue as the "cultural mandate." Anthony Hoekema, author of *Created in God's Image,* boils this mandate down to "the command to rule the earth for God, and to develop a God-glorifying culture."[2] He concludes:

> "But man—that is, we—must rule over nature in such a way as to be its servant as well. We must be concerned to conserve natural resources and to make the best possible use of them. We must be concerned to prevent the erosion of the soil, the wanton destruction of forests, the irresponsible use of energy, the pollution of rivers and lakes, and the pollution of the air we breathe. We must be concerned to be stewards of the earth and all that is in it, and to promote whatever will preserve its usefulness and beauty to the glory of God."[3]

DOMINION VS. DOMINATION

When it comes to managing our environment, *dominion* is a God-given assignment that has limitations, accountability, and rewards. *Domination* implies distortion and self-centeredness. (See the difference discussed in Ezekiel 34:5 when *radah* is used in discussing shepherds and God's flock.) The variance is great, indeed, between ruling and wrecking, but it's easy to move from ruling to wrecking if we're not careful. Why? Enter Genesis 3.

When Adam and Eve sinned, great consequences followed—both personally (death) and publicly (curses). Specifically, sin affected the earth, and Adam's experience cultivating it was forever changed (Genesis 3:17-19).

In the conditions handed down to humanity from God, there must be a healthy approach to creation that includes both ruling and serving. Not only are humans to rule and subdue the earth, but we're also "to work it and watch over it" (Genesis 2:15).*

Without thoughtful interaction toward both ruling and serving we overcompensate by either pillaging the earth carelessly or deifying it. We should neither throw rocks at the goose nor bow down and worship it. There's a better balance.

Do you feel a responsibility to watch over the earth? How does that play out in your life?

---

*Facilitator: What's the significance of Eve being created after Adam? What responsibilities for Adam does that imply of his care for Eve? How do those responsibilities compare to what Adam was asked to do in the garden?

CREATION & ESCHATOLOGY

Eschatology is the theological study of "last things," and it's generally understood to deal with matters of the end times—the second coming of Jesus, judgment, and so forth. So what does eschatology have to do with creation care?

What we believe about end times and its effect on creation has a lot to do with how we view the world right now. Many hold to the belief that God is going to destroy this world. If that notion is true, then what's the point of caring for the earth? After all, in 2 Peter 3:10-13, Peter used terms like "pass away" and even "be destroyed" to describe the end times for the earth. And verse 13 speaks of "new heavens and a new earth."

Isaiah 66:22-23 says, God will make the new heavens and the new earth. Revelation 21 continues this theme and states that "the first heaven and the first earth had passed away" (v. 1). It's easy to see how many would find the conclusion that this world is replaced with another one.

"These fascinating words suggest that the best contributions of each nation will enrich life on the new earth, and that whatever potentialities and gifts have been of value in this present life will somehow, in some way, be retained and enriched in the life to come. This implies that there will be continuity as well as discontinuity between the present life and the life to come, and that therefore our cultural, scientific, educational, and political endeavors today help us to prepare for a fuller and richer life on the new earth."[4]

The Bible indicates that God intends to "recycle" and renew this world for the life to come. Romans 8 might just be "the clearest expression of future hope for the physical world" in the New Testament.[5]

Paul has much to say about the future of creation, and he grounds his argument in human redemption (Romans 8:19-23). Paul makes the point that creation itself is longing for redemption and renewal. Just like our physical bodies will continue in the life to come—resurrected and renewed like Christ's (John 6:39-40; 1 Corinthians 15; Philippians 3:10-11; 1 John 3:2)—so will the physical creation be renewed and its original form retained. That's Paul's point, and I think it's Peter's, Isaiah's, and John's, too.

All of creation is in rebellion and under the curse of sin. Jesus gave His life to reconcile all things in heaven and on earth. Creation has suffered the consequences of human sin; however it will also enjoy the fruits of human deliverance through the atoning work of Jesus.[6]

John 3:16-17 states explicitly that God loves the world (the cosmos) and that He sent His Son to redeem and save, not to condemn and destroy. This wonderful promise is for more than just human beings; it is for the world!*

How would you answer the question, *Why should we care for the earth if God is going to make all things new?*

---

* Facilitator: Read the third stanza of the hymn "Joy to the World" for some good theology on the hope of restoration regarding creation.

How do these commands to rule and to serve help us form a proper basis for creation care? How does this balance bring glory to God?

WHAT DOES CARING FOR THE ENVIRONMENT INCLUDE?

1. Preventing air and water pollution
2. Stopping the extinction of endangered species
3. Helping bring clean water to the world
4. Assisting in protecting the world's most vulnerable from land erosion and drought
5. Controlling deforestation
6. Protecting our natural and non-renewable resources
7. Putting a stop to an ever-increasing global food crisis
8. Caring for those—humans, animals, and all living things—who cannot care for themselves

What else is on the creation care to-do list?

Scripturally we're called to rule and serve all of God's creation. So in a world of conservation issues and resource depletion, where do we begin?

SEEKING THE RIGHT BALANCE

As God-appointed managers of creation, we must find the right balance of consumption, conservation, and contribution. We can and should use the resources the earth provides, but we also need to preserve or maintain what we can for others, as well as giving back by finding ways to enrich life on earth. Let's spend some time reviewing each of these areas.

CONSUMPTION

Man is by nature a consumer for our personal necessities and desires. We're expected to use the resources God has provided in this world to meet our needs. After all, He provided an environment to please us and provide for us:

"The LORD God caused to grow out of the ground every tree pleasing in appearance and good for food, including the tree of life in the middle of the garden, as well as the tree of the knowledge of good and evil. . . . The fear and terror of you will be in every living creature on the earth, every bird of the sky, every creature that crawls on the ground, and all the fish of the sea. They are placed under your authority. Every living creature will be food for you; as I gave the green plants, I have given you everything (Genesis 2:9; 9:2-3).

Why were we given such a detailed description of all that God has put us in charge of?

_____

SESSION FOUR MANAGE

Of course, God did not intend for us to abuse and exploit the resources He provided or to fall recklessly into greed, gluttony, and hedonism. God's Word teaches against all of these sins that we've become so accustomed to.

Spending

We live in an age of great excess and easy access to indulgences beyond our necessities.* Our extravagance is staggering and grossly out of perspective compared to the majority of the world. Most of what we take for granted in basic necessities (like clean drinking water, sanitation, etc.) is absent in much of the world.[7]

Let's consider one element of our consumerist culture: how the buying power of American teenagers has changed in just eight years.

Other Scriptures on Creation
Genesis 1:20-25,31
Nehemiah 9:6
Psalm 19:1-6; 104:24
Proverbs 8:24-31
Isaiah 40:28; 45:18
Romans 8:18-23
Colossians 1:16,20
Hebrews 11:3

- In 2003, teens (ages 13-19) in the United States spent $94.7 billion.[8]
- In 2006, the same age group spent $179 billion.[9]
- Just five years later, in 2011, teenagers wielded more than $200 billion in buying power.[10]

True, the population increase plays a role in this upward trend in teen spending. But a struggling economy over those years didn't abate teens' desires for immediate gratification and a responsible engagement of the results of hard work.

Perhaps underlying ever-increasing spending and debt trends is our inability—or even unwillingness—to see that we've made justifications to support our needs versus our wants. In her book *7: An Experimental Mutiny against Excess,* Jen Hatmaker discusses this problem at length:

> "[M]arketing used to represent basic needs of humans, without much embellishment or hyperbole. Certainly, the Third World still has these needs in spades—to the detriment of life and health and family—but no consumer power. Thus, Big Marketing turned to the wallet of the privileged, invented a bunch of fake needs . . . and disregarded the people who were actually dying every

---

* Facilitator: Read Luke 11:37-42. In what ways have you focused more on your pockets and less on your heart? How do we control spending yet still maintain a generous heart?

+ Annually, more people die from unsafe water than from all forms of violence, including war.[11]

+ From 2011 to 2012, consumer food prices in the United States rose 4.4 percent.[12]

+ Nearly one in five children under age five in the developing world is underweight and malnourished.[13]

+ The rate of deforestation has increased to the equivalent of 18,100 soccer fields per day—affecting global greenhouse emissions and air quality.[14]

+ At least 80 percent of humanity lives on less than $10 a day.[15]

Which of these things surprises you most?*

day for lack of basics, exposed to the seductions of the consumer marketplace but without the means to participate in it. . . . These thoughts burden me holistically, but the trouble is, I can rationalize them individually. This one pair of shoes? Big deal. This little outfit? It was on sale. This micro-justification easily translates to nearly every purchase I've made. Alone, each item is reduced to an easy explanation, a harmless transaction. But all together, we've spent enough to irrevocably change the lives of a hundred thousand people."[16]

Consider your own consumer expenses related to food, water, clothing, housing, electronics, and entertainment. Where do you find yourself "micro-justifying"? What will you do with this information?

We discussed budgeting and spending habits in the session on money, so we won't go into more detail here. But you can see how spending habits add up—how our excess can be applied to help others who are needy. It's also important to recognize that there are other ramifications for our consumerist nature. Let's look at just one more.

Pollution

It doesn't take a degree in toxicology to know that polluting air, soil, and water is harmful to all life forms. But what many don't realize is that pollution most hurts the poor. Poverty and environmental degradation go together like beans and rice. Without adequate resources for clean water and safe shelter, "minority, low-income, and tribal populations are disproportionately exposed to and affected by pollution."[17] This fact doesn't apply to only Third World countries. In the United States alone, 37.8 percent of Americans reside

---

* Facilitator: Determine some ways your group can work together to be like Christ and help alleviate the plight of another person in need.

SESSION FOUR MANAGE

in unhealthy levels of ozone pollution.[18] More than 127 million Americans live in "counties that received an F for either ozone or particle pollution," according to the American Lung Association.[19]

A simple Google search can reveal millions of facts about the effects of plastics in ocean water, the presence of prescription drugs in our drinking water, and arsenic found in our soil. Yet studies are finding that green initiatives can make a difference. For example, in 2012 it was found that "18 of the 25 cities most polluted by ozone, including Los Angeles, had their lowest smog levels since the first State of the Air report was published in 2000."[20] And new "smart" fertilizers have prevented up to 90 percent of nutrient runoff that fouls waterways since 2001.[21] Also a weekly sweeping of street gutters (to keep free of plant residue) can lower damaging phosphorus levels by 30 to 40 percent.[22]

> "How can I be socially responsible if unaware that I reside in the top percentage of wealth in the world? (You probably do too: Make $35,000 a year? Top 4 percent. $50,000? Top 1 percent.) Excess has impaired perspective in America; we are the richest people on earth, praying to get richer."[23]
> —Jen Hatmaker, 7

So what does pollution have to do with consumption? In short, what we put in the ground, down the drain, and in the air affects all of us. Taking steps to properly dispose of chemicals and making a consistent effort to recycle and reuse as much as possible are simple steps to reducing excess and pollution.

Here's one practical example. Consider a vegetable on your dinner plate. How many miles did that vegetable have to travel before it reached your table? It's been said that food in America travels "an average of 1,500 to 2,500 miles from farm to table."[24] Those miles affect the environment in multiple ways—from the overwhelming carbon dioxide emissions to the fuel use for international and national freight. That doesn't even take into account the efforts to keep food safe (like refrigeration) and secure (like plastic packaging):

> "Distances have been increasing in recent decades, as foods increasingly are imported. If you live in Iowa, according to one study, there's a very good chance you're buying tomatoes picked 1,569 miles from your local supermarket, even though farmers grow them within 60 miles of the loading dock.

But why pick on Iowans? We've all seen those rock-hard tomatoes—and that's the second great tragedy of shipping food long distances. By the time they arrive, you forget exactly what they're supposed to taste like. And guess which tomatoes taste better and are better for you? Locally grown, of course."[25]

Just by buying produce locally, you help sustain your local farmers, reduce environmental pollution, eliminate container waste, and eat fresher, healthier foods. It's just one way to lessen our consumption while helping to conserve natural resources.*

What can you do about finding locally grown food?

My point is, it takes all of us working together to make our world safer and cleaner for our generation and those to come. If the facts aren't evidence enough that these issues are important, consider the Word of God. We're called to care for those in need:

> **"'For I was hungry and you gave Me nothing to eat; I was thirsty and you gave Me nothing to drink; I was a stranger and you didn't take Me in; I was naked and you didn't clothe Me, sick and in prison and you didn't take care of Me.'**
>
> **"'Then they too will answer, "Lord, when did we see You hungry, or thirsty, or a stranger, or without clothes, or sick, or in prison, and not help You?" 'Then He will answer them, "I assure you: Whatever you did not do for one of the least of these, you did not do for Me either"'"** (Matthew 25:42-45).

Name three practical steps you can take to begin to care for "the least of these."

---

* Be aware: "Locally grown" can be broadly defined. Wal-Mart considers anything local if it's grown in the same state as it's sold (like Texas). Whole Foods considers "local" to be anything grown within seven hours of one of its stores.[26]

Look back again at Matthew 22. Considering what you've read so far, how has your view of "Love your neighbor as yourself" changed?

To find out how many "food miles" are on your table, go to *localharvest. org/inarea.jsp.*

How can excess in our consumption, given a more godly focus, help balance the extreme needs of others?

CONTRIBUTION VIA CONSERVATION

Conservation and contribution are essential, especially since excess is so prominent in the American experience. Here's where much of the heavy lifting in creation care takes place: We effectively manage the resources we have to enrich life for us, for others, and for the earth.

Ecclesiastes 2 is an outstanding example of contributing back to creation:

> "I increased my achievements. I built houses and planted vineyards for myself. I made gardens and parks for myself and planted every kind of fruit tree in them. I constructed reservoirs of water for myself from which to irrigate a grove of flourishing trees" (vv. 4-6).

Solomon planted vineyards, made gardens and parks, planted trees, and built reservoirs of water to irrigate trees. Although he did these things for himself, he unwittingly produced a life-giving contribution through them.

Solomon is not unique among Bible characters for giving back and making good on God's intention to rule and to serve the land. Noah spent decades building an ark to retain animals and preserve them from extinction (Genesis 6:14-22). Noah guarded what was entrusted to him; he obeyed God when asked to care for His creation. In the Book of Ruth,

For more ideas on being environmentally friendly in your daily life, check out:

50waystohelp.com
blessedearth.org
heifer.org
newdream.org
arocha.org

Boaz, a wealthy relative of Ruth's deceased husband, allowed Ruth and her mother-in-law to glean from his fields behind the harvesters.

we learn about the process of gleaning, gathering grain or produce left in a field by reapers or on a vine or tree by pickers. Mosaic law required leaving a portion of what was gleaned so that the poor and aliens might have sustenance and a means of earning a living:

> "When you reap the harvest of your land, you are not to reap to the very edge of your field or gather the gleanings of your harvest. You must not strip your vineyard bare or gather its fallen grapes. Leave them for the poor and the foreign resident; I am Yahweh your God" (Leviticus 19:9-10).

What portion of your harvest are you offering to the poor?

On a trip I took to Alaska this year for king salmon fishing, I was unable to fish in the world-renowned Kenai River because the spawning levels were unusually low. At first I was frustrated, but then it dawned upon me that authorities were acting as good managers of creation: They were protecting the fish population and managing our natural resources. Once I recognized this, I happily accepted the chance to fish in a lesser-known river where the salmon were in greater abundance. Modern-day conservation efforts can be inconvenient, but that makes them no less crucial.

There are thousands of ways to contribute back to the earth and conserve what we already have. On a micro scale, this means being intentional and practical with what we can control. We can all do a better job conserving energy and making simple choices to reduce our consumption. Here are 10 practical ideas for conserving responsibly:

1. Establish a rainwater collection system for your outdoor space. Use the rainwater to water indoor plants, your grass during periods of drought, and even your garden.
2. Cut down on fast food purchases. Not only will it help your waist and your wallet, it helps eliminate the overwhelming amounts of waste from plastic containers and paper wrappers.

3. **Start a community garden.** It's healthy food and requires exercise to produce it. It can bring neighborhoods together while teaching children a life-sustaining skill.

4. **Find and use a local recycling center.** If your community doesn't offer a curbside pickup for recycling, start one. Glass, metal cans, paper products, and plastic containers can all be taken to your local recycling center. Go to *earth911.com* to find programs in your area.

5. **Use "green" cleaning products.** Household cleaners and detergents release volatile organic chemicals (VOC's) into the atmosphere, water sources, and soil. Pick the green ones instead.

6. **Buy smarter.** Use things until they wear out rather than tossing them whenever the newest version hits the market. This requires purchasing better quality clothing and shoes that can last longer. Shop at second-hand stores for "new-to-you" items at cheap prices.

7. **Buy from sustainable, fair trade programs.** Coffee is one of the most commonly purchased items worldwide. Consider the impact if all of us committed to buying coffee from an ethically traded and fair wage grower. (See some supplier ideas in "Companies with a Conscience" on p. 83.)

8. **Use less energy.** This can include installing a water shut-off valve for your shower, replacing unrepairable appliances with energy-rated ones, unplugging electronics when not in use, and using compact fluorescent bulbs. And, of course, turn off lights when you leave a room.

9. **Cut your paper goods.** Send invoices, payments, and invitations digitally. Request electronic statements when possible and recycle junk mail.

10. **Use public transportation.** It'll give you time to catch up on the latest novel you're reading and save you money on gas and car maintenance. Carpool, bike, or walk when there's an opportunity.

> List some specific steps you can take to give back to the earth for the purpose of renewal.

These ideas aren't drastic, but they're ways in which we can make a difference on a small scale. But what does this look like on a macro scale? It means being educated on global environmental issues and concerns, such as climate change, deforestation, pollution, and clean water needs. Do your own research and form some biblically based conclusions. Then pray for these issues, for the people involved, and for legislation and ministries or companies seeking to remedy such problems.

STEWARDSHIP FOR THE GOSPEL

Back to the case for balancing consumption, conservation, and contribution: We need to take ownership of our responsibility as a world citizen. There are local and global implications for how we live as consumers, and we can make an enormous impact—near and far—when we conserve and contribute back.

In fact, for us to truly feel the weight of this responsibility, we must view ecological problems and environmental issues in terms of love for our neighbors and for the promotion of the gospel.

If we proceed from this starting point and goal, how will our perceptions and choices change with respect to creation care?

ORGANIZATION SPOTLIGHT
PHOENIX COMMUNITY COFFEE

Phoenix Community Coffee is an organization that prides itself on combining great coffee with a great cause. The organization purchases coffee from missionaries around the world, paying sometimes as much as three times the fair trade price. In turn, these missionaries are able to bring relief to their migrant pickers and indigenous workers by paying them up to 400 percent more than the average farms in the area. You can find out more about Phoenix Community Coffee and learn how to get involved at *phoenixcommunitycoffee.com*.

Christopher J. H. Wright issues a provocative conclusion:

"Truly Christian environmental action is in fact also evangelistically fruitful, not because it is any kind of cover for 'real mission,' but simply because it declares in word and deed the Creator's limitless love for the whole of his creation . . . and makes no secret of the biblical story of the cost that the Creator paid to redeem both."[27]

I'm convinced that the Christian pursuit of creation care can also be evangelistically fruitful. Through simple changes and selfless choices we might demonstrate the Creator's love for all the world—His entire creation. We can accomplish the Great Commission at the same time we live out the Great Commandment.

How can sharing the gospel and caring for creation coexist in the Christian mission?

Companies with a Conscience

toms.com

warbyparker.com

thehungersite.com

thriftsmart.com

963coffee.com

themochaclub.org

saribari.com

tenthousandvillages.com

livefashionable.com

bethejoy.com

goodnewsgoods.com

3seams.com

charitywater.org

feedingamerica.org

147millionorphans.org

kiva.org

handsandfeetproject.org

THIS WEEK REFLECT ON . . .

> MAKING A CHANGE
- Start recycling and reusing. Set aside a waste-bin to fill with paper and plastics. It takes a little more effort, but you can do it!
- Instead of grabbing your favorite coffee drink every day, for one week set aside that money for one of the "Companies with a Conscience."

> GROWING WITH GOD
Spend some time reading Genesis 1–3. Make notes about God's intention for how humanity relates to creation, as well as what sin did to disrupt everything. Think about this in light of your own life, and pray about specific ways God can use you to reflect His purposes for creation.

> CLOSING QUESTIONS
- Why do you think Christians disagree or debate about how we should treat our environment?
- Do you see immediate needs in your community where you could jump in and make a contribution/difference? What's stopping you?
- How has your thinking changed on stewardship as a result of this study?

END NOTES

SESSION 1

1. "Zig Ziglar Quotes," 2012 [cited 9 August 2012]. Available from the Internet: *www.brainyquote.com.*
2. Adapted from a footnote for "Proverbs 30:7-9," HCSB Study Bible (Nashville, TN: Holman Bible Publishers, 2010), 1080.
3. Adapted from Judy Woodward Bates, "Quick tips for saving money," LifeWay.com, [cited 7 August 2012]. Available from *www.lifeway.com/Article/Quick-tips-for-saving-money.*
4. Lam Thuy Vo and Jacob Goldstein "What America Buys," NPR, April 5, 2012, [cited 7 August 2012]. Available from the Internet: *www.npr.org.*
5. "Poll: 70 Percent of American Consumers in Debt," U.S. News & World Report, July 21, 2009. Available from the Internet: *www.usnews.com.*
6. "U.S. National Debt Clock," Ed Hall [online], [cited 6 August 2012]. Available from the Internet: *brillig.com/debt_clock.*
7. Adapted from Michael Warden, "Thou Shalt Live Comfortably and Other Lies We Believe," *Collegiate,* Summer 2012, 21. Available from *www.threadsmedia.com/collegiate.*
8. "Send a Girl to School in Africa," [cited 14 August 2012]. Available from the Internet: *www.shop2give.us/HelpAfricanGirls.*

SESSION 2

1. C. S. Lewis, *The Screwtape Letters in The Complete C. S. Lewis Signature Collection* (New York, NY: HarperCollins, 2002), 176.
2. Adapted from *Biblical Illustrator,* Fall 2005, 45. © 2005 LifeWay Christian Resources of the Southern Baptist Convention. Used by permission. Available from the Internet: *www.lifeway.com/biblicalillustrator.*
3. Adapted from a footnote for "Ephesians 5:15-16," HCSB Study Bible, 2035.
4. Adapted from Gregg Matte, *Finding God's Will: Seek Him, Know Him, Take the Next Step* (Ventura, CA: Regal, 2010), 253.
5. Leland Ryken, *Redeeming the Time: A Christian Approach to Work and Leisure* (Grand Rapids, MI: Baker, 1995), 275.
6. See Nancy Pearcey, *Total Truth: Liberating Christianity from its Cultural Captivity* (Wheaton, IL: Crossway, 2004), 85-87.
7. Mark Batterson, *Chase the Lion* (Nashville, TN: LifeWay, 2007), 18.
8. Joel Drinkard, "Wealth, Trade, Money, and Coinage in the Biblical World, *Biblical Illustrator,* Winter 2003-04, 42. © 2003 LifeWay Christian Resources of the Southern Baptist Convention. Used by permission.
9. Mike Hurt, *Connect the Dots: Discovering God's Ongoing Will in Your Life* (Nashville, TN: LifeWay Press, 2008), 36.

10. "Leisure time on an average day," Bureau of Labor Statistics, American Time Use Survey, 2010. Available from the Internet: *www.bls.gov.*

11. Ibid.

12. "Percent of population who volunteered on an average day, by age," Bureau of Labor Statistics. Available from the Internet: *www.bls.gov.*

13. John Piper, *Don't Waste Your Life* (Wheaton, IL: Crossway, 2003), ch. 8.

14. Ryken, 276-277.

15. A. W. Tozer, *The Pursuit of God* (Camp Hill, PA: Christian Publications, Inc., 1993), 120-121.

16. Richard A. Swenson, *Margin: Restoring Emotional, Physical, Financial, and Time Reserves to Overloaded Lives* (Colorado Springs, CO: NavPress, 2004), 129.

17. Ibid., 128.

SESSION 3

1. Antoine de Saint-Exupéry, *Flight to Arras* (Orlando, FL: Harcourt Brace & Company, 1942), 61.

2. Adapted from Julie Hunt and Brent Hutchinson, *Relate: Knowing, loving, and forgiving the people in your life* (Nashville, TN: LifeWay Press, 2011), 7.

3. Adapted from Richard E. Dodge, "An eight-step strategy to spiritual growth," [cited 8 August 2012]. Available from the Internet: *www.lifeway. com.*

4. Dallas Willard, *The Spirit of the Disciplines* (New York, NY: HarperCollins, 1988), 158.

5. Isaac Ambrose, as quoted in Tom Schwanda, "'Hearts Sweetly Refreshed': Puritan Spiritual Practices Then and Now," *Journal of Spiritual Formation & Soul Care,* © 2010 by Institute of Spiritual Formation 2010, Vol. 3, No. 1, 21–41 Biola University, 1939-7909.

6. *Relate,* 19.

7. Thomas Merton, *The Hidden Ground of Love: Letters* (Merton Legacy Trust, 1985).

SESSION 4

1. Douglas J. Moo, "Eschatology and Environmental Ethics: On the Importance of Biblical Theology to Creation Care," in *Keeping God's Earth,* eds. Noah J. Toly and Daniel I. Block (Downers Grove, IL: InterVarsity Press, 2010), 30.

2. Anthony A. Hoekema, *Created in God's Image* (Grand Rapids, MI: Eerdmans, 1986), 14.

3. Ibid., 80.

4. Richard Mouw, *When the Kings Come Marching In* (Grand Rapids, MI: Eerdmans, 2002), 94-95.

5. Moo, "Eschatology and Environmental Ethics," 28.

6. Ibid., 30.

7. Michael Guebert, "Water for Life: Global Freshwater Resources" in *Keeping God's Earth* (Downers Grove, IL: InterVarsity Press, 2010), 143-164.

8. Nancy Wong, "Generation Y Earns $211 Billion and Spends $172 Billion Annually," Harris Interactive, [cited 14 August 2012]. Available from the Internet: *http://harrisinteractive.com.*

9. Ylan Q. Mui, "As the Kids Go Buy," The Washington Post, [cited 14 August 2012]. Available from the Internet: *www.washingtonpost.com.*

10. "30M U.S. Teens Wielding More than $200B in Buying Power," as originally reported in *www.researchandmarkets.com,* [cited 14 August 2012]. Available from the Internet: *http://pymnts.com.*

11. "World Water Day 2010," United Nations Environment Programme, [cited 10 August 2012]. Available from the Internet: *www.unep.org.*

12. Jill Priluck, "Food Fight! Stores, Producers, Consumers Battle over High Food Prices," TIME Business, [cited 9 August 2012]. Available from *http://business.time.com.*

13. "Eradicate extreme hunger and poverty: Where do we stand?" Millennium Development Goals, United Nations Development Programme, [cited 9 August 2012]. Available from the Internet: *www.undp.org.*

14. "Forest," UN Collaborative Programme on Reducing Emissions from Deforestation and Forest Degradation in Developing Countries (UN REDD), United Nations Environment Programme, [cited 9 August 2012], Available from the Internet: *www.unep.org.*

15. Shaohua Chen and Martin Ravallion, "The Developing World Is Poorer than We Thought, But No Less Successful in the Fight Against Poverty" (paper presented at Development Research Group, World Bank, Washington, D.C., August 26, 2008).

16. Jen Hatmaker, *7: An Experimental Mutiny Against Excess* (Nashville, TN.: B&H Publishing Group, 2012), 65.

17. John Collins Rudolf, January 11, 2011, "Stress, Pollution and Poverty: A Vicious Cycle?" a blog post on "Green: A Blog About Energy and the Environment," [cited 10 August 2012]. Available from the Internet: *http://green.blogs.nytimes.com.*

18. "State of the Air 2012," American Lung Association, [cited 10 August 2012]. Available from the Internet: *www.stateoftheair.org.*

19. Ibid.

20. "Air Quality Facts," American Lung Association, [cited 10 August 2012]. Available from the Internet: *www.lungusa.org.*

21. "'Smart' Fertilizer Improves Plant Growth," Penn State, Science Blog, [cited 13 August 2012]. Available from the Internet: *www.scienceblog. com.*

22. C. J. Rosen and B. P. Horgan, University of Minnesota, "Preventing Pollution Problems from Lawn and Garden Fertilizers," [cited 13 August 2012]. Available from the Internet: *www.extension.umn.edu.*

23. Hatmaker, 3.

24. Sally Deneen, "Food Miles," The Daily Green, [cited 13 August 2012]. Available from the Internet: *www.thedailygreen.com.*

25. Ibid.

26. Julie Schmit, "'Locally grown' food sounds great, but what does it mean?" USA Today, [cited 14 August 2012]. Available from the Internet: *http://usatoday.com.*

27. Christopher J. H. Wright, "'The Earth is the Lord's': Biblical Foundations for Global Ecological Ethics and Mission" in *Keeping God's Earth,* 241.

Olivia - Bryce hers
girlfriend + having
a rough time
★ Gabriella
- Hayden Renee, baby
born

★ Loving others

Alexis's mom died
+ lives w/ aunt

Jamie Cooper
- drunk
spike

texth
Christy

Katie
Drew

directions
- Grace
- Leppy
- Lydia